| TALK |

Russian

SVETLANA FURLONG
& GEORGINA MARTIN
Series Editor: Alwena Lamping

Published by BBC Active, an imprint of Educational Publishers LLP, part of the Pearson Education Group, 80 Strand, London, WC2R 0RL, England.

First published 1998.
Third edition 2015.
5 4 3 2 1

ISBN 978-1-406-68015-7

Publisher: Debbie Marshall
Project Manager: Alexis Chung
Project Editors: Tamsen Harward and Emma Brown
Edited by Anne Gibbens
Additional Editing: Sue Purcell
Illustrations: © Mark Duffin
Layout: DTP Media Ltd. www.dtp-media.co.uk
Cover design: Two Associates
Cover photograph: © iStock.com/polarica
Audio producer: John Green, tefl tapes
Sound engineer: Tim Woolf
Presenters: Larissa Kouznetsora, Leonid Osokin, Irina Shumovitch, Stanislav Suknenko
Studio: Robert Nichols Audio Productions
Music: Peter Hutchings

Printed and bound in China (CTPSC/1)

The Publisher's policy is to use paper manufactured from sustainable forests.

Contents

Introduction

Welcome to the new edition of **Talk Russian**, the bestselling course from BBC Active which has inspired and helped so many people to learn Russian from scratch and given them the confidence to have a go.

The key to **Talk Russian**'s effectiveness is the successful **Talk** method, developed by experienced teachers of languages to adult beginners. Its structured and systematic approach encourages you to make genuine progress and promotes a real sense of achievement. The choice of situations and vocabulary is based on the everyday needs of people travelling to Russia.

Talk Russian includes a book and 120 minutes of recordings of Russian native speakers. The book in this new edition has several additional features, inspired by feedback from users and teachers. There's an extended grammar section (pages 119–134) and a two-way glossary (pages 135–144), covering around 1,000 words.

Free tutors' support and activities are available online at www.bbcactivelanguages.com.

How to use Talk Russian

1 Read the first page of the unit to focus on what you're aiming to learn and set it in context while gaining some relevant vocabulary.

2 Listen to the key phrases – don't be tempted to read them first. Then listen to them again, this time reading them in your book too. Finally, try reading them out loud before listening one more time.

3 Work your way through the activities which follow the key phrases. These highlight key language elements and are carefully designed to develop your listening skills and your understanding of Russian. You can check your answers at any time in the *Transcripts and answers* starting on page 101. In the first four units new words and phrases have been transliterated (written in English letters).

Wherever you see this: **1•5**, the phrases or dialogues are recorded on the CD (i.e. CD1, track 5).

4   Read the *По-ру́сски* explanations of how Russian works as you come to them – this information is placed just where you need it.

5   After completing the activities, and before you try the *Put it all together* section, listen to the conversations straight through. The more times you listen, the more familiar Russian will become and the more comfortable you'll become with it. You might also like to read the dialogues at this stage – preferably out loud.

6   Complete the consolidation activities on the *Put it all together* page and check your answers with the *Transcripts and answers*. In the first four units these activities are specifically designed to help you to learn the alphabet.

7   Use the Russian you have learnt – the native speaker presenters on the audio will prompt you and guide you through the *Now you're talking!* page as you practise speaking Russian.

8   Check your progress. First, test your knowledge with the *Quiz*. Then assess whether you can do everything on the checklist – if in doubt, go back and spend some more time on the relevant section.

9   Read the learning hint at the end of the unit, which provides ideas and suggestions on how to use your study time effectively or how to extend your knowledge.

10 Finally, relax and listen to the whole unit, understanding what the people are saying in Russian and taking part in the conversations.

The units of **Talk Russian** have been carefully designed to cater for complete beginners, developing language in manageable steps and confining explanation of the complex grammatical structure of Russian to the essentials. For those interested in a fuller grammatical knowledge, the *Grammar* section provides a glossary of terms and more detailed explanations.

The Russian alphabet

The Russian Cyrillic alphabet has 33 letters:

Аа	a in **a**pple
Бб	b in **b**ox
Вв	v in **v**an
Гг	g in **g**et
Дд	d in **d**og
Ее	ye in **ye**t
Ёё	yo in **yo**ur
Жж	s in plea**s**ure
Зз	z in **z**oo
Ии	ee in f**ee**t
Йй	y in bo**y**
Кк	k in **k**it
Лл	l in **l**ove
Мм	m in **m**ay
Нн	n in **n**ot
Оо	o in t**o**p
Пп	p in **p**ot
Рр	r in **r**ot (rolled)
Сс	s in **s**et
Тт	t in **t**o
Уу	oo in m**oo**n
Фф	f in **f**it
Хх	ch in lo**ch** (Scottish)
Цц	ts in ve**ts**
Чч	ch in **ch**in
Шш	sh in **sh**in
Щщ	shch in pu**shch**air
ъ	hard sign (see page 36)
ы	y in ph**y**sics
ь	soft sign (see page 28)
Ээ	e in m**e**t
Юю	yu in **Yu**le
Яя	ya in **ya**p

For more information on pronunciation, go to pages 117–118.

Здра́вствуйте!

saying hello, goodbye

... and how are you?

introducing yourself

... and asking someone's name

В Росси́и ... *In Russia ...*

(Pronounced *v Rassee'ee*)

how you address someone will depend on how well you know them. You use formal language to talk to a waiter, receptionist or shop assistant or someone you don't know well, and informal language to a friend, a child or someone you know very well. Russians use a middle name formed from their father's first name: Pavel and Anna, whose father's name is Ivan, are called **Pavel Ivanovich** and **Anna Ivanovna**. Short forms of first names are common: **Ва́ня** *Vanya* is the common short form for **Ива́н** *Eevan* and **О́ля** *Olya* for **О́льга** *Olga*.

Saying hello, goodbye

1   **1•02** Listen to these key phrases.

Здра́вствуйте.	Hello. (formal)
zdrastvooytye	
Здра́вствуй.	Hello. (informal)
zdrastvooy	
До свида́ния.	Goodbye.
da sveedaneeya	

По-ру́сски … *In Russian …*
pa-roosskee …

use **Здра́вствуйте** to greet one person formally or more than
one person.

2   **1•03** Anna, a tourist guide, greets a new arrival at the hotel. Listen
and tick the word she uses to say *hello*.

Здра́вствуй   **Здра́вствуйте**

3   **1•04** Listen as Anna greets five more people in the hotel. How many
of them are young people or children?

4   **1•05** Some guests are arriving and some leaving. As you hear each
person, tick whether they are saying hello or goodbye to Anna.

	1	2	3	4	5
Здра́вствуйте					
До свида́ния					

... and how are you?

5 **1•06** Listen to these key phrases.

Как у вас дела?	How are you? (formal)
kak oo vas dyela	
Спасибо, хорошо.	Thank you, fine.
spaseeba kharasho	
А как у вас?	And you? (formal)
a kak oo vas	

6 **1•07** Listen to Anna greeting one of the tourists. Write in English what she asks him.

Спасибо,
хорошо

7 **1•08** Ivan asks Anna how she is, using **Как дела?** *kak dyela* the informal way of asking someone how they are. Listen, and give her reply in English.

8 **1•09** At a summer language school in Moscow, Olga is teaching her students to read. Pointing to phrases on the board, she reads them aloud. Listen and number the phrases 1 to 6, in the order in which she reads them.

Здравствуй	**Как у вас дела?** ....
А как у вас?	**Здравствуйте** ....
Спасибо, хорошо	**До свидания** ....

Introducing yourself

1 **1•10** Listen to these key phrases.

Меня́ зову́т …	My name is …
menya zavoot	
Как вас зову́т?	What's your name? (formal)
kak vas zavoot	

2 **1•11** Staff at the Moscow language school are introducing themselves to students. Tick the four names you hear.

Svetlana ☐   Irina ☐

Victor ☐   Yuri ☐

Tanya ☐   Olga ☐

Vladimir ☐   Ivan ☐

3 **1•12** Listen to these key phrases.

Óчень рад.	Pleased to meet you. (said by a man)
ochen rad	
Óчень páда.	Pleased to meet you. (said by a woman)
ochen rada	
Прости́те?	Pardon?/Excuse me?/Sorry?
prasteetye	

4 **1•13** Lisa, a student, doesn't quite catch her new teacher's name. Does she use **Прости́те?** or **Как вас зову́т?** to ask him to repeat it? What is his name?

Why does Lisa say **Óчень páда** *Pleased to meet you* in a different way from Victor, who says **Óчень рад**?

... and asking someone's name

5   1•14 **Áнна** *Anna* meets **Táня** *Tanya*, whose name she has forgotten. She's with her younger brother **Борúс** *Barees*. Listen to the audio and write the letter of the missing word in the appropriate gap.

Anna	**Здрáвствуйте.**
Tanya	....
Anna	**Как** .... **зовýт?**
Tanya	**Меня́ зовýт Та́ня.**
	.... **вас зовýт?**
Anna	.... **зовýт Áнна,**
	а как тебя́ зовýт?
Boris	**Меня́ зовýт Борúс.**
Anna	**Óчень рáда.**
Boris	.... **рад.**

a **Как**
b **Здрáвствуйте**
c **Óчень**
d **вас**
e **Меня́**

По-рýсски ...

to ask a child or a young person their name, use the informal **Как тебя́ зовýт?** *kak tebya zavoot* instead of **Как вас зовýт?**

---

6   1•15 Olga asks her students to do some more reading practice. Listen and number the phrases 1 to 6 in the order in which she says them.

Как вас зовýт? ....   **Как делá?** ....
Как тебя́ зовýт? ....   **Óчень рад** ....
Меня́ зовýт Áнна ....   **Простúте?** ....

put it **all together**

1   The alphabet is fun to learn and you can already recognise several letters. Concentrate now on the ones which are highlighted below.

абвгде**ё**жзий**к**л**мно**п**рсту**ф**х**цчшщъыьэ**юя**

2   **1•16** Six letters sound very similar to the English letters they look like. Listen to the audio to check your pronunciation.

Аа (a)   **Ее** (ye)   **Кк** (k)   **Мм** (m)   **Оо** (o)   **Тт** (t)

Can you now read and guess the meaning of the following words? The first two can be found in the key phrases, others in the glossary.

a	а	b	как	c	ма́ма	d	такт
e	а́том	f	ко́ма	g	ата́ка	h	коме́та

3   **1•17** Another six letters look like English but sound different:

Вв (v)   **Нн** (n)   **Рр** (r)   **Сс** (s)   **Уу** (oo)   **Хх** (kh, or ch as in loch)

Now read and guess the meaning of the following:

a	метро́	b	теа́тр	c	рестора́н	d	тра́ктор
e	курс	f	Москва́	g	орке́стр	h	хара́ктер

4   Match the Russian with the English. Write the correct letter in front of the English phrase.

a	До свида́ния.	My name's Anna.
b	Как вас зову́т?	Pleased to meet you.
c	Меня́ зову́т А́нна.	How are you?
d	О́чень рад.	Goodbye.
e	Как у вас дела́?	What's your name?

now you're talking!

1 **1•18** As you're leaving your hotel, you meet your tour guide.

- ◆ Say hello to her.
- ● **Здра́вствуйте. Как у вас дела́?**
- ◆ Say you're well and ask how she is.
- ● **Спаси́бо, хорошо́.**

Another guide joins her.

- ◆ Greet him and introduce yourself.
- ● **О́чень рад. Меня́ зову́т Ива́н.**
- ◆ He spoke very fast. Ask him to repeat his name.
- ● **Меня́ зову́т Ива́н.**
- ◆ The guides have to leave. Say goodbye to them.

2 **1•19** You're at a newspaper kiosk.

- ◆ Greet the vendor.
- ● **Здра́вствуйте.**
- ◆ Say hello to his son …
- ● **Здра́вствуйте.**
- ◆ … and ask him what his name is.
- ● **Меня́ зову́т Са́ша.**
- ◆ Now ask him how he is.
- ● **Спаси́бо, хорошо́.**

3 **1•20** Now try the following:

- ◆ Greet the waiter in a restaurant.
- ◆ Ask him his name.
- ◆ Ask him how he is.
- ◆ As you leave the restaurant, say goodbye to him.

quiz

1 Which of the following names is Anna?
   a **Ваня**   b **Таня**   c **Анна**

2 Where in Russia would you be if you were in **Москва**?

3 Who is Sasha calling '**Мама**'?

4 Where would you be if you were in a **ресторан**?

5 To say hello to a child would you use:
   a **Здравствуйте** or   b **Здравствуй**?

6 How well would you know a person to use **Как дела**?

7 To say *Pleased to meet you* would a man use:
   a **Очень рад** or   b **Очень рада**?

8 Which of the following means *Goodbye*?
   a **Здравствуйте**   b **До свидания**   c **Простите**

9 When asking a child's name do you say:
   a **Как вас зовут**? or   b **Как тебя зовут**?

10 Which of the following means *Thank you*?
   a **Спасибо**   b **Саша**   c **Хорошо**

Now check whether you can ...

- greet someone you don't know well
- greet a child
- say goodbye
- ask someone's name and give your name
- ask how someone is and say how you are
- say *Pardon?/Excuse me?/Sorry?*

Listen to the audio as often as possible. Repeat the words and phrases before you look at them in the book. Then read them after the voices. Finally, try to read them without listening to the audio. By doing this you should find that you will soon be reading Russian without any prompts.

Я англича́нин

asking someone's nationality

... and stating yours

saying whether you are married

using the numbers 0 to 4

В Росси́и ...

people are friendly and hospitable. If you can ask a few simple questions and say a little about yourself, the Russians you meet will be delighted.

Remember that if you speak Russian you should also be understood in many of the former Soviet republics, e.g. **Гру́зия** *groozeeya* (*Georgia*), **Украи́на** *ookraeena* (*Ukraine*), **Белору́ссия** *byelaroosseeya* (*Belarus*).

Asking someone's nationality

1   **1•21** Listen to these key phrases.

Вы/Ты …	Are you (formal/informal) …
vy/ty …	
… англича́нин/англича́нка?	… English (m/f)?
angleechaneen/angleechanka	
Да, я …	Yes, I am …
da ya …	
Нет, я не …	No, I'm not …
nyet ya nye …	
… англича́нин/англича́нка.	… English (m/f)

По-ру́сски …

there are no words for *am*, *is*, *are*. You simply say **я** *I* for *I am* and **вы/ты** *you* (formal/informal) for *you are*.

---

2   **1•22** Listen as Olga asks four summer school students (**студе́нты** *stoodyenty*) about themselves. Tick which nationality each of them is:

	English	American	Australian	Canadian
David				
Ann				
Lisa				
Mark				

По-ру́сски …

there are no words for *the* or *a*, but Russians do distinguish between masculine and feminine. The key is in the word ending.

Many masculine words end in a consonant (**англича́нин**, **студе́нт**), while many feminine words end in **-а** (**англича́нка**, **студе́нтка**).

... and stating yours

3 **1•23** Listen to the audio and repeat the following countries.
Can you match the English with the Russian?

a	**Аме́рика**	Russia
b	**Кана́да**	Britain
c	**А́нглия**	Australia
d	**Росси́я**	England
e	**Брита́ния**	America
f	**Австра́лия**	Canada

4 Now match the letter of the country above to the corresponding nationality below. How many are women?

1 **Я ру́сский**
ya roosskeey

2 **Я англича́нка**
ya angleechanka

3 **Я кана́дец**
ya kanadets

4 **Я америка́нка**
ya amereekanka

5 **Я австрали́ец**
ya avstraleeyets

6 **Я брита́нец**
ya breetanets

По-ру́сски ...

он *on* (*he*) also means *he is* and **она́** *ana* (*she*) also means *she is*.

---

5 Olga has written down the nationality of some of her students and fellow teachers. Give their nationality in English. Are they men or women?

	nationality		male	female
a	**Он англича́нин**	....	▢	▢
b	**Она́ америка́нка**	....	▢	▢
c	**Он ру́сский**	....	▢	▢
d	**Он кана́дец**	....	▢	▢

Saying whether you are married

1 **1•24** Listen to these key phrases.

Вы/Ты ...	Are you ...
... жена́ты/жена́т?	... married? (formal/informal,
zhenaty/zhenat	said to a man)
... за́мужем?	... married? (formal/informal,
zamoozhem	said to a woman)
Да, я жена́т/за́мужем.	Yes, I am married. (m/f)
Нет, я не жена́т/за́мужем.	No, I am not married. (m/f)

2 **1•25** Listen, and tick which students tell Olga they are married.

Дави́д ☐	**Анн** ☐	**Ли́са** ☐	**Марк** ☐
David	*Ann*	*Lisa*	*Mark*

3 **1•26** Listen to Olga introducing herself to her students, and tick the statements which are true. Listen out for the word **москви́чка** *maskveechka*, which means a woman from Moscow.

a   Her name is Olga Sergeyevna.
b   Her father's name is Ivan.
c   She is Russian.
d   She is married.

4 **1•27** She now asks her students to introduce themselves in the same way. Complete the register for her in English.

	Name	Nationality	Marital status
a			
b			
c			
d			

Using the numbers 0 to 4

1   **1•28** Listen to the following numbers.

0	1	2	3	4
ноль	**оди́н**	**два**	**три**	**четы́ре**
nol	*adeen*	*dva*	*tree*	*chetyre*

2   **1•29** Olga is teaching her summer class these numbers. Enter the figures 0 to 4 as you hear them.

a ....
b ....
c ....
d ....
e ....

3   She gives them a few simple sums. Put in the missing figure as in the example.

a   **оди́н +** 2 **= три**
b   **четы́ре −** .... **= оди́н**
c   .... **+ оди́н = два**
d   **оди́н + три =** ....

4   **1•30** Olga wants her class to do some more reading practice. Listen as she reads the following and write the numbers 1 to 8 in the order in which she reads them from the board.

Вы англича́нин?		**Да, он англича́нин**	
Вы за́мужем?		**Она́ не америка́нка**	
Ты жена́т?		**Она́ за́мужем**	
Она́ москви́чка		**Вы жена́ты?**	

put it all together

1 Focus on the highlighted letters below:

аб**в**где**ёжзи**й**к**лмнопрстуфх**ц**ч**шщ**ъы**ьэю**я**

2 **1•31 Гг** (*g*)   **Жж** (*zh*)   **Зз** (*z*)   **Ии** (*ee*)

Жж sounds like *s* in *pleasure*.

So read and guess the meaning of the following words:

a **газ**   b **газéта**   c **жест**   d **таксú**

3 **1•32 Лл** (*l*)   **Чч** (*ch*)   **ы** (*y*)   **Яя** (*ya*)

ы sounds roughly like *y* in *physics*. It can never begin a word.

So read and guess the following:

a **лигр**   b **матч**   c **вы**   d **я**

4 **1•33** See how many of these words you already know or can guess:

a **вúски**   b **килогрáмм**   c **Чéхов**   d **киóск**
e **туалéт**   f **винó**   g **москвúч**   h **москвúчка**

5 Match the Russian with the English.

a **Онá зáмужем**	He's a student.
b **Он женáт**	I'm not English. (m)
c **Онá студéнтка**	She's married.
d **Он студéнт**	He's married.
e **Я не англичáнин**	She's a student.

now you're talking!

1 **1•34** Imagine you're Maria Foster, an English student at a Moscow summer school, where you are introducing yourself to the teacher.

- ◆ Greet him.
- ● **Здра́вствуйте. Как вас зову́т?**
- ◆ Answer his question and find out his name.
- ● **Меня́ зову́т Ива́н. Как у вас дела́?**
- ◆ Say you're fine and ask if he's a Muscovite.
- ● **Да, я москви́ч.**
- ◆ Give your nationality.
- ● **О́чень рад.**
- ◆ Reply appropriately.

2 **1•35** Now imagine you're Ross Smart. Give your details to the teacher.

Name: Ross Smart.
Occupation: Student
Nationality: American
Marital status: Married

3 **1•36** Later, in the dining room, you start talking to the man sitting next to you. How would you ask him if he's:

- ◆ Russian?
- ◆ a Muscovite?
- ◆ a student?
- ◆ married?

quiz

1 Would an American woman say:
   a Я америка́нец? or **b Я америка́нка?**

2 If a man said **Я брита́нец**, where would he be from?

3 Put the numbers in the right order:
   a три   **b оди́н**   **c четы́ре**   **d два**

4 Which country would you be from if you lived in **Кана́да**?

5 What is the difference in meaning between **a да** and **b нет**?

6 Which word would you insert into the middle of **Я ру́сский**
   to say *I'm not Russian*?
   a он   **b она́**   **c не**

7 Which of the following is not a drink?
   a ви́ски   **b кио́ск**   **c вино́**

8 If a woman tells you she is **москви́чка**, where is she from?

9 Who is married – Ivan or Anna? **Ива́н не жена́т, а А́нна
   за́мужем.**

10 Name this famous writer: **Че́хов**.

Now check whether you can …

- say yes and no
- say what nationality you are
- say whether you are married or not
- ask others for this information
- use the numbers 0 to 4

Concentrate for now on understanding and reading Russian. Listen
to the audio frequently. As you don't yet know how to write Russian,
to help you learn new words and phrases you could try recording
yourself speak.

Э́то А́нна

introducing friends

... and members of your family

talking about your family

giving your phone number

using the numbers 5 to 10

В Росси́и ...

families nowadays tend to be small, generally with one or two children. The **ба́бушка** *babooshka* (*grandmother*) still plays an important role in looking after the children while the mother works. However, recently there has been a tendency towards mothers staying at home when the children are very young.

Introducing friends

1 **1•37** Listen to these key phrases.

Э́то А́нна.	This is Anna.
eta anna	
Э́то мой друг.	This is my friend. (m)
eta moy droog	
Э́то моя́ подру́га.	This is my friend. (f)
eta maya padrooga	
Э́то мой муж.	This is my husband.
eta moy moozh	
Э́то моя́ жена́.	This is my wife.
eta maya zhena	

2 Olga, the summer school teacher, introduces two of her colleagues to David, a student. Can you work out where each name belongs in the dialogue? Write the letter of the missing name in the gap.

Olga	**Э́то моя́ подру́га** ....
David	**О́чень рад.**
Olga	**Э́то мой друг** ....
David	**О́чень рад.**

a **Ле́на** (*Lyena*, a woman's name)   **b** **Лев** (*Lyev*, a man's name)

По-ру́сски ...

the word for *my* is
  мой for masculine words, e.g. **мой муж**
  моя́ for feminine words, e.g. **моя́ жена́**

---

3 **1•38** Listen to Lyena and Lyev introducing their partners to David. Tick the correct name.

Lyena's husband is:	**Ви́ктор** *Victor*	**Влади́мир** *Vladimir*
Lyev's wife is:	**Ла́ра** *Lara*	**Ли́дия** *Lydia*

… and members of your family

4   **1•39** Listen to these key phrases.

У вас есть дети?	Do you have children?
oo vas yest dyetee	
Да, у меня есть …	Yes, I have …
da oo menya yest …	
… сын	… a son
… syn	
и …	and …
ee …	
… дочь	… a daughter.
… doch	
Как его/её зовут?	What is he/she called?
kak yevo/yeyo zavoot	
Его/Её зовут …	He/She is called …
yevo/yeyo zavoot …	

Sometimes, as here, **г** is pronounced *v*.

5   **1•40** Listen as David asks if Lyena and Lyev have any children. Tick the statements which are true **да** *yes* or false **нет** *no*.

	да	нет
a Lyena has a son	☐	☐
b Lyev has a son	☐	☐

6   **1•41** David asks Olga the names of two other friends. Listen and tick the correct name.

The woman's name is:	**Наташа** *Natasha*	**Нина** *Nina*
The man's name is:	**Пётр** *Pyotr*	**Павел** *Pavel*

Talking about your family

1   **1•42** Listen to these key phrases.

Э́то ...	Is this ...
eta ...	
... ваш/твой брат?	... your brother? (formal/informal)
... vash/tvoy brat	
... ваша/твоя́ сестра́?	... your sister? (formal/informal)
... vasha/tvaya sestra	

2   **1•43** Nina and Pavel tell David about their families. Tick the statements which are true.

a   Nina has one sister.   **b**   Pavel has a daughter.

c   Nina has two brothers.   **d**   Pavel is not married.

3   Vera describes her family tree. Write the letters of the missing words in the gaps. Look up any new words in the glossary.

a	за́мужем
b	муж
c	ба́бушка
d	дочь
e	Никола́й
f	жена́т

Меня́ зову́т Ве́ра. Я за́мужем. Э́то мой .... Его́
зову́т Серге́й. У меня́ есть сын. Его́ зову́т ....
Он не .... У меня́ та́кже есть .... Её зову́т
Ири́на. Она́ .... У неё есть дочь, ита́к я ....

По-ру́сски ...

У неё/него́ есть means *she/he has*.

To ease pronunciation **н** is sometimes added to **её** and **его́**.

Giving your phone number

1   **1•44** Listen to the following numbers.

5	6	7	8	9	10
пять	**шесть**	**семь**	**восемь**	**дéвять**	**дéсять**
pyat	*shyest*	*syem*	*vosem*	*dyevat*	*dyesat*

2   **1•45** Olga is teaching her students some more numbers. Enter 5 to 10 in the order in which you hear them.

a ....   b ....
c ....   d ....
e ....   f ....

3   **1•46** David and Mark give Olga their **нóмер телефóна** *nomer telefona* (*telephone number*) while resident in Moscow. Listen and make a note of them.

David ....

Mark ....

4   **1•47** The code for Russia is 007, for Moscow 095 and for St Petersburg 812. Say the following two phone numbers out loud, giving the full code, then listen to the audio to check your answers.

Moscow	6107252
St Petersburg	3961248

5   **1•48** Olga gives her students some more reading practice. Listen, and note the order, 1 to 6, of what she reads.

Это моя подрýга ....   **Это мой муж** ....
У вас есть дéти? ....   **Это твой брат?** ....
Как его зовýт? ....   **У неё есть сын** ....

put it all together

1   Focus on the highlighted letters below:

а**б**вг**д**е**ё**жзи**й**клмно**п**рстуфхцчшщъы**ь**э**ю**я

2   **1•49** **Бб** (*b*)   **Дд** (*d*)   **Ёё** (*yo*)   **Йй** (*y*)   **Пп** (*p*)   **Ээ** (*e*)

Ёё sounds like *yo* in *your*.

й is used mainly after vowels. It sounds like *y* in *boy*.

Read and guess the meaning of the following words:

a бар   b да́ма   c её
d мой   e парк   f экза́мен

3   The letter **ь** has no sound of its own. It softens the letter before it and is known as a soft sign.
Both masculine and feminine words can end in **ь**.
Guess the meaning of: **автомоби́ль** (m)

4   **1•50** Now see how many of these words you can guess:

a дипло́м   b авто́бус   c Толсто́й
d экспе́рт   e университе́т   f трамва́й

5   Match the Russian with the English.

a	**Э́то Ви́ктор.**	I also have a son.
b	**Э́то ва́ша жена́?**	This is Victor.
c	**У меня́ та́кже есть сын.**	Have you any children?
d	**У него́ есть сын.**	What's her name?
e	**Как её зову́т?**	He has a son.
f	**У вас есть де́ти?**	Is this your wife?

1   **1•51** Imagine you're Ben Carter and the teacher at the summer school is asking you about your family. You show her the photograph below.

- ◆ Tell her you are married.
- ● **Это ва́ша жена́?**
- ◆ Say yes and give her name.
- ● **У вас есть де́ти?**
- ◆ Say you have a son and give his name.
- ● **Он жена́т?**
- ◆ Explain that he's not married but he has a daughter.
- ● **А ..., хорошо́.**

Ben

Greg

Rita   **Maria**

2   **1•52** Now imagine you are Lisa Parker. Give your details to the teacher.

Name:	..Lisa Parker..........
Occupation:	..Student...............
Nationality:	..English...............
Marital status:	..Married...............
No. of children:	..A daughter...........................
Child's name:	..Vanessa..............................

quiz

1 To say *my sister* would you use **a мой** or **b моя** in front of **сестра́**?

2 If someone asked **Это твой брат?** would they be using the formal or informal *your*?

3 Put the numbers in the right order:
   a семь   **b де́сять**   **c шесть**   **d во́семь**
   e пять   **f де́вять**

4 What would you be giving someone if you gave them your **но́мер телефо́на**?

5 Which is the odd one out?
   a авто́бус   **b парк**   **c трамва́й**

6 Name this famous writer: **Толсто́й**.

7 What does **та́кже** mean?

8 If you said **Это моя́ подру́га**, would you be introducing a male or female friend?

Now check whether you can ...

- introduce someone – male or female
- talk simply about your family/friends
- ask others for similar information
- give your phone number and use the numbers 5 to 10

A good way to practise introducing people is to use a family photograph. Point to each person and say who they are:

e.g. **Это мой брат Дави́д. Это моя́ сестра́ А́нна.**

The following words might come in useful:

ма́ма/мать *mama/mat*		mum/mother
па́па/оте́ц *papa/atyets*		dad/father
де́душка *dyedooshka*		grandfather
тётя *tyotya*, **дя́дя** *dyadya*		aunt, uncle

Чай, пожа́луйста

ordering a drink in a bar or café

offering, accepting or refusing a drink

using the numbers 11 to 20

В Росси́и ...

you can get a drink or snack in a **бар** *bar* or **кафе́** *café*, although it can be rather expensive. The **бар** is open until late at night and often has music and dancing. You place your order with the **ба́рмен** *barman*, but the **кафе́** can be self-service.

In the street you will find a **кио́ск** *kiosk* where you can buy **моро́женое** (*marozhenoye*) *ice cream*, which is very popular even in the sub-zero temperatures of winter.

Ordering a drink

1   **1•53** Listen to these key phrases.

Что вам угóдно?	What would you like?
shto vam oogodna	
Чай, пожáлуйста.	Tea, please.
chay pazhalsta	
Кóфе, пожáлуйста.	Coffee, please.
kofye	
Хорошó.	OK, that's fine.
Спасúбо.	Thank you.
Пожáлуйста.	You're welcome.

2   **1•54** Anna orders a drink in the hotel. Listen and decide whether she orders tea or coffee.

3   **1•55** The family next to her orders four different drinks. Who has what?

	водá	**винó**	**пúво**	**лимонáд**
	vada	*veeno*	*peeva*	*leemonad*
	water	wine	beer	lemonade
пáпа				
мáма				
сын				
дочь				

По-рýсски ...

all nouns are masculine (m), feminine (f) or neuter (n).

Masculine nouns usually end in a **consonant** or **й**: **лимонáд, чай**

Feminine nouns usually end in **-a** or **-я**: **водá, тётя**

Neuter nouns usually end in **-o** or **-e**: **винó, морóженое**

As there is no word for *the* or *a*, **чай** can mean *tea*, *a tea* or *the tea*.

... in a bar or café

4 **1•56** Listen as other people arrive and order drinks.

What does the man order?

Does the woman have her coffee **с сáхаром** *s sakharom* (*with sugar*) or **без сáхара** *byez sakhara* (*without sugar*)?

По-рýсски ...

the endings of nouns change in various ways after prepositions (e.g. *with, without, in, on*):

сáхар *sakhar* (*sugar*)
с сáхаром *s sakharom* (*with sugar*)
без сáхара *byez sakhara* (*without sugar*)

For the moment just learn these as set phrases.

---

5 **1•57** How does Tanya order her coffee? Does she want any sugar?

a with milk (**с молокóм** *s malakom*)
b without milk (**без молокá** *byez malaka*)

6 **1•58** Listen as Ivan orders tea, and decide whether he wants it with sugar, milk or lemon.

7 **1•59** Does Victor order sparkling (**с гáзом** *s gazom*) or still (**без гáза** *byez gaza*) mineral water?

8 **1•60** How would you ask for:

- a beer?
- a coffee with milk?
- tea without sugar?

Offering, accepting or refusing a drink

1   **1•61** Listen to these key phrases.

Что вы хоти́те?   What would you like (formal)?
shto vy khateetye

Что ты хо́чешь?   What would you like (informal)?
shto ty khochyesh

… а вы/ты?   … and for you (formal/informal)?

Да, пожа́луйста.   Yes, please.

Нет, спаси́бо.   No, thank you.

2   **1•62** Anna is in the hotel bar. Listen as she offers one of the visitors a drink.

What does he ask for?

When he thanks her, which of the following words does Anna use to say *You're welcome*?

  a **Хорошо́.**   b **Пожа́луйста.**   c **Спаси́бо.**

3   **1•63** Katya and Misha, two of Anna's colleagues, come into the bar, so she offers them a drink too. Katya wants a fruit juice (**сок** *sok*). What does Misha order? Which phrase does Anna use to Katya and why?

  a **Что вы хоти́те?**   b **Что ты хо́чешь?**

По-ру́сски …

вы *you* is used to address more than one person, as well as one person in a formal situation.

Sometimes the word for *you* is left out altogether:
Что хо́чешь? *What would you like?*

Using the numbers 11 to 20

1 **1•64** Olga has taken her summer school class out for the day. Ten of the students have already set off with two other teachers. Listen as she does a head count of the others.

11	оди́ннадцать	16	шестна́дцать
12	двена́дцать	17	семна́дцать
13	трина́дцать	18	восемна́дцать
14	четы́рнадцать	19	девятна́дцать
15	пятна́дцать	20	два́дцать

2 **1•65** They all go into a café and Olga has to order for everyone. Listen to her order and fill in the number of drinks and ice creams ordered:

Лимона́д ....

Пе́пси-ко́ла ....

Моро́женое ....

3 **1•66** Back in class, Olga gives her students some number practice. Write down in the spaces the numbers that you hear.

a .... **b** .... **c** .... **d** .... **e** ....

4 She also asks them to put the following dialogue in the correct order. Can you? Number the phrases one to five appropriately.

Конья́к, пожа́луйста.
Что ты хо́чешь?
Пожа́луйста.
Конья́к? Хорошо́.
Спаси́бо.

put it all together

1   Once you've studied the following highlighted letters, you'll have reached the end of the Russian alphabet! **Браво!** *Well done!*

абвгдеёжзийк**л**мнопрсту**ф**х**ц**ч**шщъ**ыь**э**ю**я

2   **1•67 Фф** (*f*)   **Цц** (*ts*)   **Шш** (*sh*)   **Щщ** (*shch*)   **Юю** (*yu*)

   Цц sounds like *ts* in *pets*
   Щщ sounds like *shch* in *pushchair*

   So read and guess the meaning of the following words:

   a фа́нта   b центр   c шампа́нское   d борщ   e меню́

3   **1•68** Like the soft sign **ь**, the hard sign **ъ** has no sound of its own and is rarely used. Between a consonant and a vowel, it can indicate a slight pause between the two sounds. Listen to the pronunciation of **съезд**, which means *congress*, and **объе́кт**, which you can probably guess. If not, you'll find the answer on page 105.

4   **1•69** You now have the Russian alphabet under your belt, so have some fun reading and translating the following:

   **a администра́тор   b телефо́н   c конце́рт
   d Чайко́вский   e Росси́я   f Санкт-Петербу́рг**

5   Match the Russian with the English.

a	**Пи́во, пожа́луйста.**	Coffee without sugar.
b	**Что вам уго́дно?**	Tea with milk.
c	**Чай с молоко́м.**	You're welcome.
d	**Ко́фе без са́хара.**	A beer, please.
e	**Пожа́луйста.**	What would you like?

now you're talking!

1 **1•70** You're attending a conference in St Petersburg with
Andrey, a Russian business colleague, whom you've got to
know very well.

- ◆ In the bar you ask him what he'd like to drink.
- ● **Пи́во, пожа́луйста.**
- ◆ As you are about to order, his wife, whom you've only met
  once before, joins you both. Ask her what she'd like.
- ● **Пе́пси-ко́ла, пожа́луйста.**
- ◆ Now greet the barman and order a beer, a coke and a
  lemonade.

2 **1•71** Now imagine you're in a café in Novgorod.

- ◆ Greet the waitress.
- ● **Здра́вствуйте. Что вам
  уго́дно?**
- ◆ Order a tea.
- ● **С са́харом?**
- ◆ Say with sugar but no milk.
- ● **Хорошо́.**
- ◆ When the drink arrives,
  thank the waitress.
- ● **Пожа́луйста.**

3 **1•72** Try the following:

- ◆ Ask your good friend Igor if he wants a coffee.
- ◆ Ask if he wants the coffee with sugar.
- ◆ Check if he wants it with milk.
- ◆ Finally, order his coffee with milk but no sugar.

quiz

1 Which is the odd one out?
   a сáхар   b молокó   c чай   d кóфе

2 Which alcoholic drink would you get if you ordered **конья́к**?

3 Put the numbers in the right order:
   a восемнáдцать   b семнáдцать   c девятнáдцать

4 Give the three English meanings of **кóфе**.

5 Are nouns ending in **-о** masculine, feminine or neuter?

6 What would you get with your tea if you ordered **чай с лимóном**?

7 What would you get if you ordered **морóженое**?

8 If you asked for **минерáльная водá без гáза** would you get still or sparkling mineral water?

9 Who is the **бáрмен**?

Now check whether you can …

- order a drink in a bar/café
- offer someone a drink
- accept or refuse politely when someone offers you a drink
- say whether you want your drink with or without something
- use the numbers 11 to 20

Now that you've completed the alphabet, go back to the beginning of the book and read all the Russian words and phrases you've met so far. Check your pronunciation with the recordings.

Don't worry at this stage about making mistakes or about words changing their endings, e.g. **сáхар/с сáхаром**. If you know the basic word you'll be able to make yourself understood. As you gain confidence, you'll find it easier to focus on the detail.

Контро́льная рабо́та 1

1 **1•73** Olga is interviewing one of her summer school students. Listen, and tick the details that match what he tells her.

Ро́бин Мо́рсон	англича́нин ☐	австрали́ец ☐
Он	жена́т ☐	не жена́т ☐
У него́ есть	сын ☐	дочь ☐
Его́ зову́т	Кри́стиан ☐	Кри́стофер ☐

2 **1•74** David, one of the students, has become friendly with a Russian student, Anton, who has invited him to his flat in Moscow. Listen, then fill in the missing details in English.

David meets Anton's .... and ....

Anton's sister's name is ....

She says she is ....

David is from ....

3 **1•75** Listen as Anton offers David a drink. Tick the drink he is *not* offered.

a пи́во   b вино́   c лимона́д   d ко́фе   e чай

4 **1•76** Read the names of these drinks aloud, then check your pronunciation with the audio. Look up the meaning of any you don't understand in the glossary.

во́дка	конья́к	фа́нта	чай	тома́тный сок
лимона́д	вино́	джин	ко́фе	шампа́нское
ви́ски	ром	молоко́	вода́	пе́пси-ко́ла

5 **1•77** From your study of the alphabet you'll have noticed that words of more than one syllable have a stress mark, which in turn affects the pronunciation of the other vowels. See if you can read and understand the names of these countries. Then check your pronunciation with the audio, paying particular attention to how the word is stressed.
Look up any words you're unsure of in the glossary.

Ирла́ндия	Уэ́льс	Шотла́ндия
Ита́лия	Испа́ния	Фра́нция
Гре́ция	Болга́рия	Герма́ния

6 Match the questions with the answers.

1	Как вас зову́т?	a	Да, я за́мужем.
2	Вы англича́нка?	b	Его́ зову́т Ива́н.
3	Вы за́мужем?	c	Да, пожа́луйста, с са́харом.
4	У вас есть де́ти?	d	Спаси́бо, хорошо́.
5	Как его́ зову́т?	e	Чай, пожа́луйста.
6	Как у вас дела́?	f	Да, у меня́ есть сын.
7	Что вам уго́дно?	g	Нет, я ру́сская.
8	Вы хоти́те ко́фе?	h	Меня́ зову́т Ири́на.

7 Add the following numbers and write the answer in figures.

a шестна́дца́ть + трина́дцать = ☐
b четы́рнадцать + пять = ☐
c семь + восемна́дцать = ☐
d два́дцать + оди́ннадцать = ☐
e двена́дцать + девятна́дцать = ☐

8 Choose the expression that fits each context.

1 In reply to **Как дела?**
2 The opposite of **Нет**.
3 You haven't heard something properly.
4 In reply to **Спасибо**.
5 Saying *Goodbye*.
6 You're introduced to someone.

a Простите?

b До свидания

c Очень рад

d Да

e Спасибо, хорошо

f Пожалуйста

9 Write the letter of the missing word in the appropriate gap.

1 Это Бен. Он ....   a Иван
2 У .... есть сестра.   b американка
3 .... зовут Ольга.   c англичанин
4 Очень ....   d меня
5 Меня зовут ....   e рад
6 .... у вас дела?   f Её
7 Это Никола. Она ....   g Как

Take the first letter of each missing Russian word to find the name of a country.

10 Elizabeth, a friend's daughter, has received the following letter from a Russian pen friend. The letter is typed but Masha has handwritten the beginning and her name. Can you translate it for Elizabeth? Any words you're unsure of can be found in the glossary.

Дорогая Элизабет

Меня́ зову́т Ма́ша. Я москви́чка. Я студе́нтка в Москве́. Мой па́па инжене́р и моя́ ма́ма гид. У меня́ есть сестра́. Её зову́т Ната́ша. Она́ шко́льница. У меня́ та́кже есть ба́бушка. Мой но́мер телефо́на: 007 095 1670355. До свида́ния.

Ма́ша

дорога́я (f) *dear*
инжене́р *engineer*
гид *guide*
шко́льница *schoolgirl*
в *in*
и *and*

You should be very proud of how much Russian you can read, understand and speak already. Don't try to write Russian yet – if you compare the printed and handwritten words from Elizabeth's letter, you will see that some letters look very different.

Дорога́я Элизабет   *Дорогая Элизабет*

Ма́ша   *Маша*

Скажи́те, пожа́луйста, где гости́ница?

asking where something is

... and how far it is

asking where someone lives

using the numbers 21 to 199

В Росси́и ...

many of the towns are rich in history, with beautiful squares, boulevards and interesting buildings. If you visit a **музе́й** *museum* you will find it packed with foreign and Russian tourists alike. **В Москве́** *in Moscow* be sure to go to the **Кремль** *Kremlin*, while **в Санкт-Петербу́рге** *in St Petersburg* no trip would be complete without a visit to the **Эрмита́ж** *Hermitage Museum*.

Asking where something is

1 1•78 Listen to these key phrases.

Прости́те, пожа́луйста.	Excuse me, please.
Скажи́те, пожа́луйста.	Tell me, please.
Где?	Where?
Где гости́ница?	Where is the hotel?
Где рестора́ны?	Where are the restaurants?
Иди́те ...	Go ...

... пря́мо

... нале́во   ... напра́во

2 **1•79** Listen as Lisa asks Olga where the following places are. Say where she wants to go in English, and tick the direction she should take.

		left	straight on	right
a	по́чта			
b	метро́			
c	теа́тр			
d	гости́ница			
e	рестора́н			
f	музе́й			

По-ру́сски ...

nouns change their endings for the plural. There are a variety of endings which you will need to learn at a later stage. One of the most common endings is: **ы**

Где гости́ницы?	*Where are the hotels?*
Где рестора́ны?	*Where are the restaurants?*

... and how far it is

3 **1•80** Listen to these key phrases.

Это далеко?	Is it far?
Да, далеко.	Yes, it's a long way.
Нет, недалеко.	No, it's not far.
Десять минут пешком.	Ten minutes on foot.
Пять минут автобусом.	Five minutes by bus.
Один километр.	One kilometre.

4 **1•81** Lisa now asks Olga if the places are far away. Listen and fill in the distance. Then tick whether she is told to go by bus or on foot.

		on foot	by bus
a	The theatre is .... minutes	▢	▢
b	The museum is .... minutes	▢	▢
c	The post office is .... minutes	▢	▢
d	The hotel is .... minutes	▢	▢
e	The restaurant is .... minutes	▢	▢
f	The underground is .... minutes	▢	▢

По-русски ...

the words for *one* are **один** (m), **одна** (f), **одно** (n)

Два *two* only has two forms: **два** (m, n) and **две** (f)

From two onwards, nouns change their endings after numbers:

masculine	feminine	neuter
один километр	**одна минута**	**одно место** *place*
два километра	**две минуты**	**два места**
пять километров	**пять минут**	**пять мест**

These rules take time to get used to – for the moment, just concentrate on understanding the number and the noun.

Asking where someone lives

1   1•82 Listen to these key phrases.

Где вы живёте?	Where do you live (formal)?
Где ты живёшь?	Where do you live (informal)?
Я живу́ …	I live …
… в Санкт-Петербу́рге.	… in St Petersburg.
… в Но́вгороде.	… in Novgorod.
… в Волгогра́де.	… in Volgograd.

2   1•83 Listen to Olga asking some of her students where they live. Write down their home town in English.

Lisa   ....

David   ....

Mark   ....

Ann   ....

3   1•84 Olga asks two colleagues to tell her class if they live in Moscow. Listen, and write their replies in English, then tick the name of the colleague she knows quite well.

Лев   ....

Пётр   ....

По-ру́сски …

after **в** *in* nouns usually change their ending to **-е** (sometimes to **-и**):

Петербу́рг	**в Петербу́рге** *in (St) Petersburg*
Москва́	**в Москве́** *in Moscow*
Росси́я	**в Росси́и** *in Russia*

Some don't change at all, e.g. **в метро́** *in the underground*.

Using the numbers 21 to 199

1 **1•85** Listen to the following numbers.

21	**двáдцать одúн**	40	**сóрок**
22	**двáдцать два**	50	**пятьдесят**
23	**двáдцать три**	60	**шестьдесят**
24	**двáдцать четы́ре**	70	**сéмьдесят**
25	**двáдцать пять**	80	**вóсемьдесят**
26	**двáдцать шесть**	90	**девянóсто**
27	**двáдцать семь**	100	**сто**
28	**двáдцать вóсемь**	101	**сто одúн**
29	**двáдцать дéвять**	110	**сто дéсять**
30	**трúдцать**	142	**сто сóрок два**
31	**трúдцать одúн**, etc.	199	**сто девянóсто дéвять**

2 **1•86** Olga shows her class the following envelope and reads it aloud.

She explains that **Кудá** indicates where the letter is going and **Комý** tells us who it is being sent to.

г./гóрод	*town*
ул./ýлица	*street*
д./дом	*house/block*
кв./квартúра	*flat*

Listen to these people from Tverskaya Street and fill in the number of the block and flat in which they live. The first one has been done for you.

a д. **13** кв. **89**   b д. ☐ кв. ☐
c д. ☐ кв. ☐   d д. ☐ кв. ☐

put it all together

1   You are turning into **у́лица Чéхова** from **Тверска́я у́лица**. Where are the following places situated? Write the letters in the right places on the map.

   a Теа́тр напра́во   **b Пóчта налéво**   **c Метрó пря́мо**

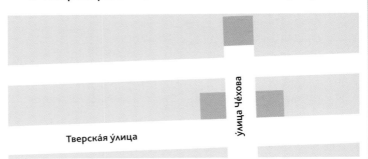

2   Work out the following times and distances:

   a   три́дцать пять киломéтров
   b   пятьдеся́т одна́ мину́та
   c   со́рок во́семь мину́т
   d   девяно́сто две мину́ты
   e   шестьдеся́т оди́н киломéтр
   f   во́семьдесят три киломéтра

3   Unscramble the letters to find the following:

   a   a town
   b   a number
   c   a form of transport
   d   a direction

   у́гПтеребр
   кроóс
   ро́тме
   я́рмоп

4   Match the questions to the answers:

1	Где музéй?	a	Нет, пять мину́т автóбусом.
2	Э́то далекó?	b	Нет, в Нóвгороде.
3	Где ты живёшь?	c	Иди́те напра́во.
4	Вы живёте в Москвé?	d	Я живу́ в Манчéстере.

now you're talking!

1 **1•87** Outside the hotel you see Anna, the tour guide. You need to ask her where a few places are.

- ◆ Say *Excuse me* and ask her where the underground is.
- ● Метро́? Иди́те нале́во.
- ◆ Ask if it's far.
- ● Нет, пять мину́т пешко́м.
- ◆ Now ask her where the post office is.
- ● По́чта? Иди́те пря́мо.
- ◆ Thank her.

2 **1•88** Imagine you're Mike Simpson on holiday in St Petersburg. You're looking a bit lost when a friendly Russian approaches you.

- ● Вы ру́сский?
- ◆ Say no, you're American, and ask if he's Russian.
- ● Да, я ру́сский.
- ◆ Ask him if he lives in St Petersburg.
- ● Да. Где вы живёте?
- ◆ Tell him you live in New York.
- ● А ..., хорошо́.
- ◆ Ask him to direct you to the Hermitage Museum.
- ● Эрмита́ж? Иди́те нале́во и пря́мо.
- ◆ Ask if it's far.
- ● Нет, де́сять мину́т пешко́м.
- ◆ Thank him and say goodbye.

quiz

1 If you were told to go **напра́во**, would you go left or right?

2 Would you put **a оди́н** or **b одна́** in front of **по́чта** to explain that there is one post office in your town?

3 Which word would not be used for *Excuse me*?

    a Иди́те   **b Прости́те**   **c Скажи́те**

4 What is the difference in meaning between:

    a теа́тр and   **b теа́тры**?

5 If you travel by bus do you go:

    a пешко́м?   **b авто́бусом**?

6 Where would you live if you lived **в кварти́ре**?

7 Which of the following numbers is not divisible by five?

    a сто   **b пятьдеся́т пять**   **c со́рок два**

Now check whether you can ...

- ask where something is
- ask if it's far
- understand basic directions
- say where you live
- ask someone where they live
- use the numbers 21 to 199

Practise your Russian at every opportunity. As you walk down any street, say the house numbers to yourself. When you're in town, try to name the places you know in Russian. Whenever you change direction say **нале́во, пря́мо** or **напра́во** to yourself.

Remember, don't worry about words changing their endings – just memorize the basic word to make yourself understood.

Это открыто?

understanding what there is in town

... and when it's open

making simple enquiries

asking for help to understand

В России ...

to obtain **информа́ция** *information* about a town and its amenities, ask at the **се́рвис-бюро́** *service desk* in a hotel. This should be easy to locate as it now usually has the sign in English: **INFORMATION**. All large and even some small hotels give you details of tourist attractions and opening times of museums, theatres and shops. Museum opening times vary but many shops are open seven days a week. The sign **Выходно́й день** *day off* tells you on which days things are closed.

Understanding what there is in town

1   **2•01** Listen to these key phrases.

Вот …	Here's …
… план го́рода.	… a map of the town.
Здесь есть …	Here, there is/are …
… банк.	… a bank.
Здесь нет …	Here, there isn't/aren't …
в це́нтре	in the centre

2   Can you match the Russian words below with the English equivalents? Many are very similar and you will probably be able to guess the meaning, others you may have to look up in the glossary. Some resemble words from other languages.

банк	магази́н
библиоте́ка	универма́г
апте́ка	суперма́ркет
кино́	бассе́йн
буфе́т	парк
галере́я	ры́нок

park	gallery
snackbar	department store
bank	cinema
swimming pool	supermarket
shop	library
market	chemist's

3   **2•02** Anna tells a group of tourists about some of the amenities **в го́роде** *in town*. She mentions a few of the places from the list above. Tick them as you hear them. Where will you find a bank?

По-ру́сски …

after **нет** *there isn't/aren't* nouns change their endings:

нет ба́нка (m)   **нет апте́ки** (f)   **нет вина́** (n)

Add -а or -я for masculine and neuter singular, -ы or -и for feminine. Many neuter nouns don't change, e.g. **нет кафе́**.

... and when it's open

4   **2•03** Listen to these key phrases.

Это откры́то?	Is it open?
Это откры́то.	It's open.
Это закры́то.	It's closed.
сего́дня	today
se<u>v</u>odnya	

понеде́льник *Monday* **пн**	**четве́рг** *Thursday* **чт**
вто́рник *Tuesday* **вт**	**пя́тница** *Friday* **пт**
среда́ *Wednesday* **ср**	**суббо́та** *Saturday* **сб**
	воскресе́нье *Sunday* **вс**

По-ру́сски ...

days of the week are often seen in their abbreviated form.

To say *on* a particular day of the week use **в**: **в четве́рг**. Feminine names of days change their ending from **-а** to **-у**: **в сре́ду**

5   **2•04** Tanya is teaching her students the days of the week. She points to places on a map. Listen and decide whether the place is open or closed, and fill in the day in English.

	откры́то	**закры́то**	day
a	☐	☐	....
b	☐	☐	....
c	☐	☐	....

Making simple enquiries

1 **2•05** Listen to these key phrases.

Есть …?	Is/are there …?
Здесь есть …?	Is/are there … here?
Прости́те.	Excuse me./Sorry.
Я не зна́ю.	I don't know.

2 **2•06** Listen as Tanya asks in the café if there's a phone and a toilet, and decide whether the following are true or false.

		да	нет
a	**Здесь есть туале́т**	☐	☐
b	**Туале́т напра́во**	☐	☐
c	**Нет телефо́на**	☐	☐

3 **2•07** Later in the street she asks a passer-by the way. Which of the following words does he use to say he doesn't know?

a **Я не ру́сский**   b **Я не жена́т**   c **Я не зна́ю**

4 **2•08** She tries again. Listen out for **пото́м** *then*. Make a note of the instructions in English. Where does she want to go, and is it open?

По-ру́сски …

to say *it is* simply use **он** (m) **она́** (f) **оно́** (n)
to say *they are* use **они́**

You can turn these into questions without changing the word order, just by adding a question mark and making it <u>sound</u> like a question.
Она́ откры́та? *Is it* (f) *open?*
Они́ в це́нтре? *Are they in the centre?*

... and asking for help to understand

5 2•09 Listen to these key phrases.

Повторите, пожалуйста.	Please repeat that.
Говорите, пожалуйста, медленно.	Speak slowly, please.
Я не понимаю.	I don't understand.

6 2•10 David, one of Olga's students, is in the town centre, asking the way. Listen, and fill in the letters of the missing words in the gaps. **на улице Чехова** means *in Chekhov Street*.

David	................, пожалуйста, где здесь библиотека?
Passer-by	В центре, на улице Чехова.
David	Простите, я не понимаю.
	Повторите, пожалуйста.
Passer-by	Библиотека в ...., на улице Чехова.
David	Спасибо. Она открыта во вторник?
Passer-by	Да, она ....
David	А здесь есть банк?
Passer-by	Есть.
David	Он открыт?
Passer-by	Нет, сегодня ....
David	Говорите, пожалуйста,
	....
Passer-by	.... банк закрыт.
David	Спасибо.
Passer-by	....

- a открыта
- b Сегодня
- c Пожалуйста
- d Скажите
- e медленно
- f центре
- g закрыт

По-русски ...

открыт and **закрыт** must agree with the word they describe, i.e. take a masculine, feminine or neuter form:

буфет открыт	аптека открыта	кафе открыто
буфет закрыт	аптека закрыта	кафе закрыто

put it all together

1 Read the following notices and answer the questions.

> **Третьяко́вская галере́я**
>
> метро́: Третьяко́вская
> откры́та: вт–вс 10.00–18.30
> выходно́й день: понеде́льник

> **Музе́й Пу́шкина**
>
> метро́: Кропо́ткинская
> откры́т: вт–пт 10.00–16.00
>   сб–вс 12.00–18.00

> **Апте́ка Фармако́н**
>
> метро́: Тверска́я
> откры́та: пн–сб 08.30–20.00

   a On which day is the Tretyakov Gallery closed?
   b When is the Pushkin Museum open from 10.00 to 16.00?
   c When is it open on Sundays?
   d On which day is the chemist's closed?

2 Say which of the amenities mentioned in this unit there are in your home town.
   e.g. **Есть парк, по́чта, ...**

3 Can you say in Russian on which days the following are open and closed in your town?

   a swimming pool   b library   c post office

1   **2•11 В го́роде** *in town*, you stop a man in the street to ask for some information.

- ◆ Say *Excuse me* and ask if there's a department store here.
- ● **Да, есть, на у́лице Пу́шкина.**
- ◆ Say you don't understand and ask him to repeat what he said.
- ● **Да, есть, на у́лице Пу́шкина.**
- ◆ Ask him if the department store is open.
- ● **Да, он откры́т.**
- ◆ Thank him and ask if there's a chemist's here.
- ● **Апте́ка? Иди́те напра́во, пото́м пря́мо.**
- ◆ Ask him to speak slowly.
- ● **Апте́ка – напра́во, пото́м пря́мо.**
- ◆ Repeat the instructions and then ask if it's open.
- ● **Да, она́ откры́та.**
- ◆ Thank the man.
- ● **Пожа́луйста.**

2   **2•12** Now imagine you're showing a Russian business colleague a map of your town. You'll need to be able to:

- ◆ say *Here's a map of the town*
- ◆ tell him the shops are in the centre
- ◆ say there is a market here on Thursday
- ◆ tell him that the post office is closed on Sunday
- ◆ say that there isn't a bank here.

quiz

1 If you were told **Банк в це́нтре**, where would you find a bank?

2 If the **библиоте́ка** is **закры́та**, would the library be open or closed?

3 What would you have if someone gave you a **план го́рода**?

4 Which word should you use with **апте́ка** to say that it's closed?
  a **закры́т**   b **закры́та**   c **закры́то**

5 Put the following days of the week in order:
  a **четве́рг**   b **пя́тница**   c **среда́**

6 According to this sign, on which day is the shop closed?
Выходно́й день: воскресе́нье.

7 What is the Russian for *Repeat*?
  a **Повтори́те** or b **Говори́те**

Now check whether you can ...

- tell someone what there is in a town
- ask if something is available
- ask if a place is open or closed
- say you're sorry, you don't know
- ask someone to repeat something and to speak slowly
- recognize the names of the days of the week

Learning a new language often involves guessing the meaning of words. It doesn't always work, but it's worth a try. You may be pleasantly surprised at how many Russian words sound similar to English and other languages.

Суперма́ркет is an example of a word recently adopted into the Russian language. **Макдо́нальдс** is now a popular eating place for many Russians. Can you guess what it is?

Ско́лько сто́ит?

using the numbers above 200

understanding prices

asking for items in a shop or market

В Росси́и ...

if you go to the **универса́м** *self-service shop* or many of the large new department stores, you may not need to speak a lot of Russian. However, in small towns you will still find traditional stores, where shopping can be quite a long process. You choose your goods at the counter, where you'll be told **Плати́те в ка́ссу** *Pay at the cash desk*. You tell the cashier what you intend to buy and say the price. You'll then be given a **чек** *receipt*, which you finally take back to the counter to receive your purchases.

Using numbers above 200

1 **2•13** Listen to the following numbers.

200	двести	900	девятьсот
300	триста	1000	тысяча
400	четыреста	2000	две тысячи
500	пятьсот	3000	три тысячи
600	шестьсот	4000	четыре тысячи
700	семьсот	5000	пять тысяч
800	восемьсот	6000	шесть тысяч, etc.

В России …

the currency is the **рубль** or **р.** *rouble*. There are 100 kopecks (**копейка** or **к.**) in a rouble.

---

2 Match the Russian price with the correct figures.

a **пять рублей двадцать две копейки**
b **сорок один рубль пятнадцать копеек**
c **тысяча триста шестьдесят три рубля**

> 41р. 15к.
> 1 363р.
> 5р. 22к.

3 **2•14** Listen to the audio and write the prices you hear.

a .... **р.** .... **к.**   b .... **р.** .... **к.**   c .... **р.** .... **к.**

По-русски …

after 1 and compounds of 1 use **рубль** and **копейка**:
21р. = двадцать один рубль; 41к. = сорок одна копейка

after 2, 3, 4 and their compounds use **рубля** and **копейки**:
32р. = тридцать два рубля; 43к. = сорок три копейки

after all other numbers use **рублей** and **копеек**.

... and understanding prices

4 **2•15** Listen to these key phrases.

Ско́лько сто́ит?	How much is it?
Ско́лько сто́ят?	How much are they?
У вас есть ...?	Have you got ...?
Да́йте (мне), пожа́луйста, ...	Could you give me ...?

5 Anna is going shopping. Read her shopping list and find out what she needs, using the glossary.

откры́тка
почто́вая ма́рка
аспири́н
фотоаппара́т
шампа́нское
сувени́ры

6 **2•16** First, she goes into the **апте́ка**. Listen, note what she buys, and give the price.

7 **2•17** Next, to **ГУМ** *GUM*, a huge department store in Moscow, to buy something for her father's birthday. Listen and find out how much the two items cost, then circle the correct price tag.

шампа́нское

600р.

800р.

700р.

фотоаппара́т

6225р.

4330р.

2465р.

8 **2•18** Finally, listen to Anna in the **по́чта** and answer these questions:

- how much is a postcard?
- how many does she buy?
- how much is a stamp for America (**в Аме́рику**)?

Asking for items in a shop

1   **2•19** Listen to these key phrases.

Мо́жно?	May I?
Мо́жно посмотре́ть?	May I have a look?
Мо́жно.	Yes, you may./It's possible./OK.
Что ещё?	Anything else?
Э́то всё.	That's all.

2   **2•20** Mark is looking for something typically Russian to take home to Australia. Listen to the conversation and decide which of the following Russian souvenirs he buys.

шáпка   **икрá**   **матрёшка**

ло́жки   **во́дка**

3   **2•21** Listen to Mark at the cash desk (**ка́сса**). How much does he pay for the souvenir? What does the cashier give him as well as his change (**сда́ча**)?

4   **2•22** How would you ask if the shop has the following, and if you can look at it/them? Listen and follow the example.

- painted wooden spoons
  У вас есть ло́жки? Мо́жно посмотре́ть?
- vodka
- caviar
- a set of Russian dolls
- a Russian hat

... or market

5 Anna goes to the market. Read her shopping list and label the food shown above with the correct letter. Use the glossary if necessary.

a **хлеб (батóн)**
b **я́блоки (килогрáмм)**
c **помидóры (полкилó)**
d **сыр (двéсти пятьдеся́т грамм)**
e **молокó (пакéт)**

6 **2•23** Listen as Anna speaks to various traders **на ры́нке** *at the market*, and number the items on her list as you hear them. What does she forget to buy?

По-рýсски ...

nouns change their endings when they follow numbers and quantities. It is possible to avoid these changes by saying the item first, e.g.:

Помидóры – килогрáмм, пожáлуйста.
Я́блоки – три, пожáлуйста.

put it **all together**

1   Write the following numbers in figures.

   a   ты́сяча девятьсо́т семна́дцать
   b   семь ты́сяч четы́реста девяно́сто шесть
   c   два́дцать две ты́сячи пятьсо́т во́семьдесят три
   d   пятьсо́т ты́сяч сто пятьдеся́т пять

2   Match the English with the Russian phrases.

a	Мо́жно посмотре́ть?	How much is it?
b	Да́йте, пожа́луйста, ...	That's all.
c	Э́то всё.	How much are they?
d	Ско́лько сто́ит?	Have you got ...?
e	У вас есть ...?	Could you give me ...?
f	Что ещё?	May I have a look?
g	Ско́лько сто́ят?	Anything else?

3   Unscramble the conversation by numbering these phrases 1 to 5.

   пятьдеся́т рубле́й – килогра́мм.
   Да́йте, пожа́луйста, полкило́.
   Ско́лько сто́ят?
   Да, есть.
   У вас есть помидо́ры?

4   Write the following shopping list in English.

   сыр – сто пятьдеся́т грамм
   бато́н – два
   помидо́ры – четы́ре
   минера́льная вода́ – литр
   я́блоки – полкило́

now you're talking!

1   **2•24** Imagine you're in **ГУМ**, looking for a Russian souvenir to take home.

- ◆ Greet the assistant and ask if they have any souvenirs.
- ● **Да. Что вы хотите?**
- ◆ Say you don't know.
- ● **Вот, пожалуйста, ложки или матрёшка.**
- ◆ Ask if you can have a look (at them).
- ● **Можно. Вот, пожалуйста.**
- ◆ Ask the price of the spoons.
- ● **Двести рублей.**
- ◆ Find out the cost of the set of Russian dolls.
- ● **Семьсот рублей.**
- ◆ You decide on the spoons. Ask for them.
- ● **Хорошо. Это всё?**
- ◆ Say yes, that's all thank you.
- ● **Платите в кассу двести рублей.**

2   **2•25**

- ◆ Go to the cash desk, say *spoons* and give the price.
- ● **Пожалуйста, чек.**
- ◆ Thank the cashier.
- ● **Пожалуйста.**

3   **2•26**

- ◆ Back at the counter, say *Here's the receipt*.
- ● **Пожалуйста, ложки.**
- ◆ Thank the assistant.
- ● **Пожалуйста.**

quiz

1 Would you use **a Ско́лько сто́ит?** or **b Ско́лько сто́ят?** to ask the price of **Я́блоки-четы́ре?**

2 Would you put **a рубль** **b рубля́** or **c рубле́й** after the number **сто четы́ре?**

3 How many **копе́йки** are there in a **рубль?**

4 What sort of shop is **ГУМ?**

5 If you are told **Плати́те в ка́ссу**, where should you go?

6 If you wanted a loaf of bread, would you ask for:
a паке́т or **b бато́н?**

7 To ask *Is that all?* would the sales assistant say:
a Мо́жно?   **b Ско́лько?**   **c Э́то всё?**

Now check whether you can ...

- use the numbers above 200
- ask how much something costs
- understand prices and simple quantities, e.g. a kilo, a carton
- ask for something in a shop or market
- ask if you can look at something

When Russians speak, you may not always hear the noun ending clearly, but you'll understand the basic word. Similarly, you shouldn't worry about getting the ending wrong. You'll learn much more quickly by trying to express yourself, even if you make a few mistakes, than by saying nothing until you're word-perfect.

You can give yourself time to think by saying, for example:
Как сказа́ть по-ру́сски? *How do you say in Russian?*

Контро́льная рабо́та 2

1 **2•27** Listen to three people outside the Astoria Hotel being given directions. Follow their route on the map. In the spaces below write down in English the places they're looking for, and then put the corresponding letters in the correct boxes above.

a ....   b ....   c ....

2 **2•28** Now listen and say whether the places they're looking for are open or closed.

a ....   b ....   c ....

3 2•29 Listen and check whether the prices you hear are the same as the ones on the list. Tick the ones that are correct and change the ones that are wrong.

во́дка – литр	240р
молоко́ – паке́т	48р
хлеб – бато́н	34р
сыр – 300г	100р
помидо́ры – полкило́	22р

4 Look at the envelope below, which has been addressed in the handwritten script. See if you can recognise any words and select the right answers below, before looking back at the printed envelope on page 47.

Куда́: г. Москва

ул. Тверская

д. 15 кв. 52

Кому́: Иванову П. А.

a	The town is:	Moscow	Minsk
b	The apartment number is:	15	52
c	The addressee is:	Petrov	Ivanov

5 Unscramble the anagrams to find:

- **a** a day of the week
- **b** something you're given at the **ка́сса**
- **c** a place to live
- **d** something worn on the head

асбубтеó
кче
ркатрáйв
пкашá

6 Which one would you use …

- **a** Повтори́те, пожа́луйста.
- **b** Я не понима́ю.
- **c** Как сказа́ть по-ру́сски?
- **d** Э́то далекó?
- **e** Я не зна́ю.

1 … to say you don't understand?
2 … if you don't know something?
3 … to find out how to say something in Russian?
4 … when you'd like to hear something again?
5 … to ask if something's far away?

7 Match each sentence to the place in which you're most likely to hear it.

- **a** Скóлько стóит ма́рка в Аме́рику?
- **b** У вас есть аспири́н?
- **c** Пи́во, пожа́луйста
- **d** Мóжно посмотре́ть сувени́ры?
- **e** Я́блоки – килогра́мм, пожа́луйста

1 апте́ка
2 пóчта
3 ры́нок
4 бар
5 ГУМ

8   David has gone to spend a few days in St Petersburg. Read the
    postcard he sends to Mark, using the words below to help you.
    Then decide whether the statements which follow are true or false.

Дорого́й Марк,

Как дела́?
Сего́дня воскресе́нье. И вот я в
Санкт-Петербу́рге. Я живу́ в
гости́нице 'Спорт', на у́лице
Толсто́го. В гости́нице есть
бассе́йн и са́уна. Недалеко́ –
музе́й, галере́я и кино́, пять мину́т
авто́бусом, и та́кже краси́вый парк.
В це́нтре есть магази́ны,
универма́г, суперма́ркет и ры́нок.
Приве́т.   **Дави́д**

АВИА
PAR AVION

РОССИЯ

г. *Москва*

ул. ...

д. ...

Ива...

Дорого́й	*dear* (m)
на у́лице Толсто́го	
in Tolstoy Street (talstova)	
са́уна	*sauna*
краси́вый	*beautiful*
Приве́т	*Regards*

		да	нет
a	Дави́д в Но́вгороде.	☐	☐
b	Он в гости́нице.	☐	☐
c	Гости́ница на у́лице Че́хова.	☐	☐
d	В гости́нице есть са́уна.	☐	☐
e	Недалеко́ есть музе́й.	☐	☐
f	Недалеко́ есть та́кже библиоте́ка.	☐	☐
g	В це́нтре ры́нок.	☐	☐

You'll find that sometimes Russian uses far fewer words than
English, e.g. **Недалеко́ есть музе́й**, where only three words are
needed to say *Not far away there is a museum.*

Have you also noticed that some Russian words have several
meanings?

Пожа́луйста. *Please./Don't mention it./Here you are./After you.*
Мо́жно? *Is it possible?/May I?/Can we?*
Мо́жно. *Yes, you may./It's possible./By all means./OK.)*

У вас есть свободный номер?

checking in at reception

asking if there's a room free

asking which floor something is on

making requests

В России ...

it is much easier to travel independently than it used to be and it is just as common to do so as to use organised package tours. **Интурист** *Intourist* still runs many hotels, but there are a large number of big international and private Russian hotels. Some enterprises even offer accommodation in private homes, an ideal way to **говорить по-русски** *talk Russian*. If you book a **номер люкс** *luxury room*, your room will be more like an apartment with a sofa, TV, fridge and a separate bedroom.

Checking in at reception

1   **2•30** Listen to these key phrases.

| Я заказа́л ... | I've booked ... (man speaking) |
| Я заказа́ла ... | I've booked ... (woman speaking) |

... но́мер люкс

... одноме́стный но́мер

... двухме́стный но́мер

с ва́нной

с ду́шем

Ва́ша фами́лия, пожа́луйста.	Your surname, please.
Ваш па́спорт, пожа́луйста.	Your passport, please.
Вот мой па́спорт.	Here's my passport.

2   **2•31** Anna is in reception, helping some guests to check in. Listen and fill in their room details in English below.

	Type of room	**Bath/shower**
Brown		
Smith		
Anderson		

По-ру́сски ...

after **с** *with*, singular nouns usually change as follows:
add **-ом** or **-ем** to masculine and neuter nouns
add **-ой** or **-ей** to feminine nouns
с са́харом (m)   **с ва́нной** (f)   **с вино́м** (n)

Asking if there's a room free

1 **2•32** Listen to these key phrases.

У вас есть свобо́дный но́мер?	Have you got a room free?
Како́й но́мер …	What sort of room …
… вы хоти́те?	… do you want?
На ско́лько челове́к?	For how many people?
На ско́лько дней?	For how many days?
На оди́н день.	For one day.
На два/три/четы́ре дня.	For two/three/four days.
На пять/семь дней.	For five/seven days.

2 **2•33** Listen to these people, who have arrived at the hotel without a reservation. Look at their **анке́та** *registration form* and tick the correct information. **Коли́чество** means *number*.

> **Анке́та**
>
> **фами́лия:** ..Гага́рин/Каре́нин........
> **коли́чество челове́к:** ..оди́н/два......................
> **коли́чество дней:** ..три/четы́ре................
> **но́мер:** ..с ва́нной/с ду́шем........

> **Анке́та**
>
> **фами́лия:** ..Петро́ва/Ивано́ва........
> **коли́чество челове́к:** ..два/три.........................
> **коли́чество дней:** ..пять/семь....................
> **но́мер:** ..с ва́нной/с ду́шем........

Asking which floor something is on

1   2•34 Listen to these key phrases.

На како́м этаже́?	On which floor?
на пе́рвом этаже́	on the ground (literally 1st) floor
на второ́м этаже́	on the first (literally 2nd) floor

В Росси́и ...

they use the same system as the Americans to refer to different floors. When you are **на пе́рвом этаже́** (literally, *on the 1st floor*) you are at ground level.

на тре́тьем этаже́	*on the second (3rd) floor*
на четвёртом этаже́	*on the third (4th) floor*
на пя́том этаже́	*on the fourth (5th) floor*
на деся́том этаже́	*on the ninth (10th) floor*

2   Which floors are these rooms on?

a **на восьмо́м этаже́** ....   b **на двена́цатом этаже́** ....

c **на шесто́м этаже́** ....   d **на девя́том этаже́** ....

3   2•35 Listen to Anna telling some guests where their rooms are. Match each person to the correct floor.

1	Бра́ун	a	**на седьмо́м этаже́**
2	Смит	b	**на оди́ннадцатом этаже́**
3	А́ндерсон	c	**на пе́рвом этаже́**

По-ру́сски ...

пе́рвый *first*, **второ́й** *second*, etc. change their ending, as do nouns, depending on their function in a sentence. After **на** *on* before masculine or neuter nouns the ending is usually -ом (**на пе́рвом этаже́**) and before feminine nouns -ой (**на пе́рвой у́лице**).

Making requests

1   **2•36** Listen to these key phrases.

Мо́жно ...	Is it possible to/May I/we ...
... **посмотре́ть но́мер?**	... look at the room?
... **пообе́дать в гости́нице?**	... dine in the hotel?
... **заказа́ть такси́?**	... book a taxi?
Мо́жно оплати́ть ...	May I/we pay ...
... **креди́тной ка́ртой?**	... by credit card?
... **до́лларами/фу́нтами?**	... with dollars/pounds?

2   **2•37** Listen to three people talking to the **Администра́тор** *Manager* in the hotel and answer the questions.

a   How does the first guest want to pay?
b   Where is the taxi rank (**стоя́нка такси́**)?
c   On which floor is the room offered to the second guest?
d   Where is the lift (**лифт**)?
e   Can the third guest dine in the hotel?

По-ру́сски ...

Мо́жно, used on its own, means *May I/we?* or *You may*.
It can be followed by a verb in the infinitive (the dictionary form, usually ending in -ть), e.g. **Мо́жно пообе́дать?**
It can also be used with a noun to ask for something e.g.:
Ключ мо́жно? *May I/we have the key?*

put it all together

1   Unscramble the following conversation by numbering the phrases 1 to 8.

Да, есть. На ско́лько дней?
Мо́жно. Вот ключ.
И на ско́лько челове́к?
На три дня.
У вас есть свобо́дный но́мер?
Мо́жно посмотре́ть но́мер?
На два.
Есть двухме́стный но́мер на седьмо́м этаже́.

2   Find the most suitable rooms for these hotel guests.

1   **Я заказа́л номер с ду́шем.**
2   **Я заказа́ла но́мер с телефо́ном.**
3   **Я заказа́л одноме́стный но́мер.**
4   **У вас есть но́мер люкс?**
5   **Мо́жно посмотре́ть но́мер с ванной?**

a   c   e

b   d

3   Match the answers with the questions.

1	На ско́лько дней?	a	Но́мер с ва́нной.
2	Рестора́н на како́м этаже́?	b	На пять дней.
3	Како́й но́мер вы хоти́те?	c	Нет, до́лларами.
4	Мо́жно посмотре́ть но́мер?	d	Да, мо́жно. Вот ключ.
5	Мо́жно оплати́ть фу́нтами?	e	На второ́м этаже́.

now you're talking!

1 **2•38** Take the part of **Мария Ивановна Петрова,** arriving at the **Гостиница Спутник.**

◆ Greet the manager and ask if they have a room free.
● **Одноместный или двухместный номер?**
◆ Say *A single room with a shower.*
● **На сколько дней?**
◆ Say *For two days.*
● **Хорошо. Есть свободный номер на пятом этаже.**
◆ Ask if you can see the room.
● **Можно. Вот ключ.**

2 **2•39** You have decided to take the room, so you return to reception.

● **Ваша фамилия, пожалуйста.**
◆ Give your surname.
● **Ваш паспорт, пожалуйста.**
◆ Say *Here's my passport.*
● **Спасибо.**
◆ Ask if you can dine in the hotel.
● **Да, ресторан открыт.**
◆ Find out on what floor the restaurant is.
● **На третьем этаже.**
◆ Ask if you can pay by credit card.
● **Да, можно.**
◆ Thank him.
● **Пожалуйста.**

quiz

1 Would a man say **a Я заказа́л** or **b Я заказа́ла**?

2 If someone asked you for your **па́спорт**, what would you give them?

3 If your room was **на пе́рвом этаже́** of a Russian hotel, would you be on the ground floor or first floor?

4 Who is the **Администра́тор** in a hotel?

5 If you were asked to complete an **анке́та**, what would you be given to fill in?

6 Where would you be if you were in a **лифт**?

7 If you told someone your **фами́лия**, what would you be telling them?

Now check whether you can ...

- say you've booked a room
- ask if there's a room free
- specify the type of room you want
- say how long you want the room for
- ask which floor something is on
- ask to see the room
- ask about methods of payment

Looking up Russian words in a dictionary can at times seem confusing. For example, if you look up the word **но́мер** you'll find that it has several meanings:
number (of a telephone);
room (at a hotel);
size (of clothes);
item (at a concert).

You can usually work out the correct meaning from the context.

Когда́ отхо́дит?

asking about public transport

finding out train times

buying train tickets

finding your way around the Metro

В Росси́и ...

there is a wide choice of public transport in towns. You can take a **трамва́й** *tram*, **тролле́йбус** *trolleybus* or **авто́бус** *bus*. When you buy a **тало́н** *ticket*, you can travel any distance for the same price.

In Moscow and St Petersburg, as well as in some of the former Soviet republics, the **метро́** *underground* is an excellent way to travel.

You might like to use the **по́езд** *train* to travel longer distances, and even go on the Trans-Siberian Express, the ultimate way to see Russia!

Asking about public transport

1   **2•40** Listen to these key phrases.

Есть автобус до ...?	Is there a bus to ...?
Есть автобус до метро?	Is there a bus to the Metro?
Какой автобус ...	Which bus ...
трамвай ...	tram ...
троллейбус ...	trolleybus ...
... идёт до ...?	... goes to ...?

2   **2•41** Listen to three people outside their hotel asking how to get to various places. Write down in English how they intend to travel, the number of the bus, tram or trolleybus, and where they want to go. Listen for the word **остановка** (bus, tram or trolleybus stop).

	Form of transport	Number	Destination
a			
b			
c			

По-русски ...

до means *to* (*up to*, *as far as*), and nouns that follow **до** usually change their endings as follows:
masculine and neuter singular nouns to **-а** or **-я**
до ресторана   to the restaurant
feminine singular nouns to **-ы** or **-и**
до почты   to the post office

Words originating from other languages, e.g. **метро**, do not change.

---

3   **2•42** Listen to the audio. How would you ask:

- if there's a bus to the airport (**аэропорт**)?
- which trolleybus goes to the railway station (**вокзал**)?
- which tram goes to Pushkin Street (**улица Пушкина**)?

Finding out train times

1 2•43 Listen to these key phrases.

Когда́ отхо́дит?	When does it leave?
В кото́ром часу́ …	At what time …
… сле́дующий по́езд …	… is the next train …
… до Москвы́?	… to Moscow?
Когда́ я бу́ду в Москве́?	When will I be in Moscow?

По-ру́сски …

the twenty-four hour clock is widely used. To say at what time
something happens, begin with в *at* and use the same endings for **час**
hour as for **киломе́тр** on page 45.

в час `01:00` **в три часа́** `03:00` **в два́дцать часо́в** `20:00`

в трина́дцать часо́в со́рок мину́т `13:40`

---

2 Write the following times in numbers.

a **два́дцать оди́н час пятна́дцать мину́т**
b **семна́дцать часо́в два́дцать одна́ мину́та**
c **два́дцать два часа́ со́рок три мину́ты**
d **шесть часо́в три́дцать пять мину́т**

3 2•44 Listen to people at the **спра́вочное бюро́** *enquiry office* asking
about train times, and fill in the missing departure and arrival times.

	Отправле́ние *Departure*	Прибы́тие *Arrival*
Оде́сса		
Я́лта		
Ки́ев		

Buying train tickets

1   2•45 Listen to these key phrases.

Один билéт/два билéта до …	One/two tickets to …
Билéт в одúн конéц …	A single ticket …
… úли тудá и обрáтно?	… or return?
С какóй платфóрмы …	From which platform …
… отхóдит пóезд?	… does the train leave?

2   2•46 Listen to four people buying train tickets and decide whether they want a single or return.

	в одúн конéц	тудá и обрáтно
Москвá	▢	▢
Нóвгород	▢	▢
Одéсса	▢	▢
Сóчи	▢	▢

3   2•47 Listen to these passengers at the **спрáвочное бюрó** asking which platform they need. Make a note in English of their destinations and the platform numbers.

	Destination	Platform
a		
b		
c		
d		

Finding your way around the Metro

1 **2•48** Listen to these key phrases.

Сле́дующая ста́нция …	The next Metro station is …
Вот схе́ма метро́.	Here's a plan of the Metro.
Где мо́жно купи́ть биле́т?	Where can I buy a ticket?
На́до …	Do you/I have to …
… де́лать переса́дку?	… make a change?
Когда́ на́до выходи́ть?	When do I have to get off?

2 **2•49** Mark is travelling on the Moscow underground for the first time. He isn't sure where he has to go to buy a ticket, so he asks a Russian woman, who is very helpful and accompanies him on the train. Listen and decide whether the following statements are true or not.

	да	нет
a На́до идти́ нале́во		
b На́до де́лать переса́дку		
c Сле́дующая ста́нция Ки́евская		

3 **2•50** On the train, Mark hears some announcements, which tell him the station he's at, to be careful as the doors are closing and the name of the next station:

> **Ста́нция Ба́уманская … Осторо́жно, две́ри закрыва́ются.**
> **Сле́дующая ста́нция Сре́тенский Бульва́р.**

Listen, and as you hear them, number 1 to 4 each station he arrives at.

Пло́щадь Револю́ции	……………………
Смоле́нская	……………………
Ки́евская	……………………
Арба́тская	……………………

put it **all together**

1   Select the answer for each question.

1	Где мóжно купи́ть билéт?	a	Троллéйбус нóмер три́дцать.
2	С какóй платфóрмы отхóдит пóезд?	b	Есть. Вот напрáво – останóвка.
3	Какóй троллéйбус идёт до Эрмитáжа?	c	Нáдо купи́ть в кáссе.
4	Какóй билéт вы хоти́те?	d	В оди́н конéц, пожáлуйста.
5	Есть автóбус до метрó?	e	С платфóрмы нóмер шесть.

2   Work out how you would say the following in Russian, using the twenty-four hour clock.

a   at 01.00   b   at 13.00
c   at 04.00   d   at 16.00
e   at 07.10   f   at 19.10

3   Choose the correct ending for each sentence.

1	Осторóжно, двéри	a	Арбáтская.
2	Нáдо дéлать	b	отхóдит в семь часóв.
3	Пóезд до Ки́ева	c	девянóсто рублéй.
4	Слéдующая стáнция	d	закрывáются.
5	Билéт стóит	e	пересáдку.

4   Unscramble the letters to find four forms of transport.

a   вóсбаут
b   дóзпе
c   лртблйсéуо
d   ймтавáр

now you're talking!

1 2•51 Imagine you're outside your hotel, talking to your guide. She has just recommended a visit to the **Арба́т**, a popular shopping precinct in the centre of Moscow.

◆ Ask if it's far.
● **Нет, де́сять мину́т тролле́йбусом.**
◆ Ask which trolleybus.
● **Тролле́йбус но́мер два́дцать шесть.**
◆ Find out where the trolleybus stop is.
● **Иди́те нале́во, там остано́вка.**

2 2•52 After your visit to the **Арба́т**, you decide to travel back on the Metro.

◆ At the enquiry office, ask where Kievskaya station is.
● **Вот схе́ма метро́ и вот – Ки́евская.**
◆ Ask if you have to change.
● **Нет, не на́до.**

3 2•53 The next day you want to travel to St Petersburg on the overnight train.

◆ At the ticket office, ask for a single ticket to St Petersburg.
● **Две ты́сячи шестьсо́т рубле́й.**
◆ Find out the time of the next train.
● **В два́дцать два часа́.**
◆ Ask what platform the train leaves from.
● **С платфо́рмы но́мер двена́дцать.**

quiz

1 What type of transport would you use at the **аэропо́рт**?
2 Why would you go to the **спра́вочное бюро́**?
3 What is the difference between a **вокза́л** and b **ста́нция метро́**?
4 If you were at an **остано́вка**, which of the following would you *not* be waiting for?

   a **трамва́й**   b **по́езд**   c **тролле́йбус**

5 What sort of ticket is a **биле́т туда́ и обра́тно**?
6 If you are told **На́до де́лать переса́дку**, what would you need to do?
7 Is a **схе́ма метро́** a a metro ticket b a metro station or c a map of the metro?
8 Which is the most appropriate answer to the question **Когда́ отхо́дит по́езд?** a **В два часа́ со́рок мину́т** or b **С платфо́рмы но́мер семь**?

Now check whether you can ...

- ask which tram, trolleybus or bus goes to a particular place
- ask what time trains (or other means of transport) depart
- find out when you'll be in a particular place
- find out what platform a train leaves from
- ask for a single or return ticket
- find out if you have to change
- understand announcements on the Metro

When learning a language it can be very easy to underestimate how much you know. Go back occasionally to one of the early units to prove to yourself how much you've learnt. Remember how difficult the word **Здра́вствуйте** seemed when you first met it. A good tip to help you 'Talk Russian' is to paraphrase, i.e. simplify what you want to say, and avoid saying anything too complicated.

Приятного аппетита!

reading the menu

asking what's available

ordering a meal

saying what you like and don't like

В России ...

there is a wide choice of eating places, from fast-food outlets to designer restaurants, and eating out is becoming more and more popular. If you dine in a more traditional **ресторан** it will almost certainly have an **оркестр** and a dance floor.

A number of restaurants offer **традиционная русская кухня** *traditional Russian cooking*, while others specialise in **национальные блюда** *national dishes* from one of the regional restaurants such as the **Узбекистан** *Uzbekistan*. It is also common to find restaurants offering **Европейская кухня** *European cuisine*.

In a restaurant, you will often be wished **Приятного аппетита!** *Enjoy your meal!*

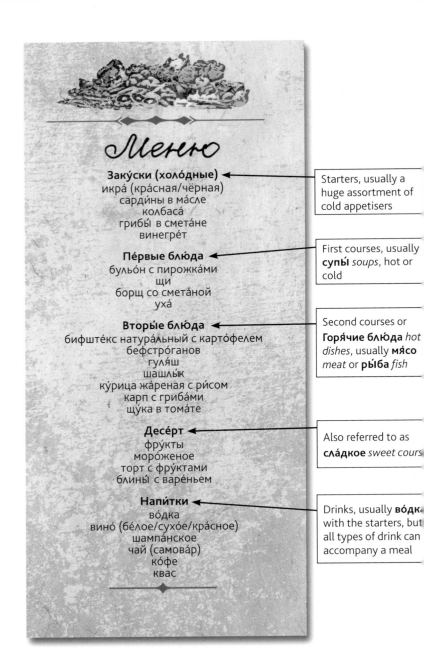

Меню

Заку́ски (холо́дные)
икра́ (кра́сная/чёрная)
сарди́ны в ма́сле
колбаса́
грибы́ в смета́не
винегре́т

Starters, usually a huge assortment of cold appetisers

Пе́рвые блю́да
бульо́н с пирожка́ми
щи
борщ со смета́ной
уха́

First courses, usually **супы́** *soups*, hot or cold

Вторы́е блю́да
бифште́кс натура́льный с карто́фелем
бефстро́ганов
гуля́ш
шашлы́к
ку́рица жа́реная с ри́сом
карп с гриба́ми
щу́ка в тома́те

Second courses or **Горя́чие блю́да** *hot dishes*, usually **мя́со** *meat* or **ры́ба** *fish*

Десе́рт
фру́кты
моро́женое
торт с фру́ктами
блины́ с варе́ньем

Also referred to as **сла́дкое** *sweet cours*

Напи́тки
во́дка
вино́ (бе́лое/сухо́е/кра́сное)
шампа́нское
чай (самова́р)
ко́фе
квас

Drinks, usually **во́дка** with the starters, but all types of drink can accompany a meal

Reading the menu

Read through the following notes, then read the menu. Consult the glossary for any words you can't guess.

Drinks and dishes are often described by adjectives, which have to agree with the noun they describe:

бифште́кс натура́льный (m)	*beefsteak* – grilled
кра́сная икра́ (f)	*red caviar* (cheaper than black caviar)
бе́лое вино́ (n)	*white wine*
холо́дные заку́ски (plural)	*cold starters*

The following adjectives are worth knowing:

горя́чий	*hot*	**жа́реный**	*fried/roasted*
чёрный	*black*	**сла́дкий**	*sweet*

Usually the main course comes already garnished (**с гарни́ром**) but sometimes the vegetables or sauce may be specified using:

с *with* + endings on page 72 – or
в *in* + endings on page 46.

чай с лимо́ном (m)	*tea with lemon*
борщ со смета́ной (f)	*beetroot soup with sour cream*
блины́ с варе́ньем (n)	*pancakes with jam*
карп с гриба́ми (pl)	*carp with mushrooms*
щу́ка в тома́те (m)	*pike in tomato sauce*
грибы́ в смета́не (f)	*mushrooms in sour cream*
сарди́ны в ма́сле (n)	*sardines in oil/butter*

Traditionally, for dessert, Russians often heat the **самова́р** and drink **чай** with **варе́нье** *jam*.

Asking what's available

1   2•54 Listen to these key phrases.

Да́йте, пожа́луйста, меню́.	Give me a menu, please.
Каки́е заку́ски у вас есть?	What starters have you got?
Что у вас есть сего́дня …	What have you got today …
… на пе́рвое?	… for the first course?
… на второ́е?	… for the main course?
… на десе́рт?	… for dessert?

2   2•55 Anna and Ivan are in the **Моско́вский** restaurant. Listen out for the polite way to call the waiter, **Молодо́й челове́к**, and write down in English what they ask him for.

3   2•56 Listen as they ask what starters are available today, and number the items as you hear them. Listen out for the word **то́лько** *only*. Which of their starters is not available?

a   кра́сная икра́   b   чёрная икра́
c   сарди́ны в ма́сле   d   колбаса́
e   грибы́ в смета́не   f   винегре́т

4   2•57 They ask what soup there is. Listen and say what sort of soup Anna wants.

5   2•58 Listen as the waiter tells them what's on offer for the main course and say whether the following are true or false:

	да	нет
a Есть шашлы́к		
b Есть щу́ка с гриба́ми		
c Есть ку́рица с карто́фелем		
d Есть бефстро́ганов		

Ordering a meal

1   **2•59** Listen to these key phrases.

Слу́шаю вас.	At your service. (I'm listening.)
Что вы рекоменду́ете?	What do you recommend?
Что вы бу́дете есть?	What will you have to eat?
Что вы бу́дете пить?	What will you have to drink?
Счёт, пожа́луйста.	The bill, please.

2   **2•60** Another customer at the restaurant is ready to order his meal. Listen as he calls the waitress, **Де́вушка**. Tick what he orders from the menu on page 88.

По-ру́сски ...

feminine singular nouns, e.g. **ку́рица**, change their ending from **-а** to **-у** when they are the object of a verb:

Да́йте мне ку́рицу.	*Give me the chicken.*
Да́йте мне матрёшку.	*Give me the set of dolls.*

Here **ку́рицу** and **матрёшку** are the objects of the verb *give*.

Что вы бу́дете есть?	*What will you have to eat?*
Ку́рицу, пожа́луйста.	*Chicken, please.*

Here **ку́рицу** is the object of the verb *I'll have/eat*.

---

3   **2•61** Listen as the same customer orders a drink and say in English what he asks for. Circle the Russian word he uses.

    Во́дка   **Во́дку**

4   **2•62** After his meal he asks for the bill. Listen, and choose the correct amount below:

a   **2500 рубле́й**   b   **2750 рубле́й**   c   **1750 рубле́й**

Saying what you like

1   2•63 Listen to these key phrases.

Мне нра́вится …	I like …
Вам нра́вится …?	Do you like …? (formal)
Тебе́ нра́вится …?	Do you like …? (informal)

2   2•64 A family in the **Салю́т** Restaurant are having a meal. Listen as they discuss the main courses, and draw a line to match each person to the dish they like.

мáма   пáпа (Ми́ша)   сын (Пётр)   дочь (Натáша)

a **ры́ба**   b **бифште́кс**   c **бефстро́ганов**   d **карп**

По-ру́сски …

to talk about liking something which is plural, you replace **нра́вится** with **нра́вятся** but they sound very similar.

Вам нра́вятся сарди́ны?	*Do you like sardines?*
Тебе́ нра́вятся грибы́?	*Do you like mushrooms?*
Да, мне нра́вятся.	*Yes, I like them.*

---

3   2•65 How would you say you like the following? Check with the audio.

- caviar
- pancakes
- red wine
- cold starters

... and don't like

4 **2•66** Listen to these key phrases.

Мне не нра́вится ...	I don't like ...
Мне о́чень нра́вится ...	I like ... very much.
Мне бо́льше нра́вится ...	I prefer ...
Э́то о́чень вку́сно.	This is/It's very tasty.

5 **2•67** Listen as the waiter begins to take their order for starters and write down in English what the mother orders.

6 **2•68** The father and son now choose their starters. Listen out for the word **коне́чно** *of course*, and tick the dish they ask for.

па́па: **винегре́т/сала́т**
сын: **кра́сная икра́/чёрная икра́**

7 **2•69** Listen and note down in English why the daughter doesn't want a starter. Listen out for the word **ничего́** *nothing*, which is a useful little word, also used to mean *not bad/never mind*.

8 **2•70** The **метрдоте́ль** *head waiter* comes to ask if everything is all right: **Всё норма́льно?** Listen and fit the letter of the missing word into the appropriate gap.

a нра́вится	**c вку́сно**
b Всё	**d Да**

Метрдоте́ль	.... норма́льно?
Па́па	................., спаси́бо.
Метрдоте́ль	Тебе́ .... десе́рт?
Пётр	Да, э́то о́чень ....

put it **all together**

1   Match the English with the Russian phrases.

a	с варéньем	fried
b	в томáте	with mushrooms
c	жáреный	in butter
d	в мáсле	tasty
e	с гарнúром	with jam
f	с грибáми	garnished with vegetables
g	вкýсно	in tomato sauce

2   Put the letters for the following dishes in the correct columns.

закýски	пéрвые блюда	вторы́е блюда	десéрт
…………	…………	…………	…………
…………	…………	…………	…………
…………	…………	…………	…………

a   торт   b   шашлы́к   c   кýрица   d   икрá
e   щýка   f   я́блоки   g   борщ   h   морóженое
i   щи   j   винегрéт

3   How would you say you like the following?

a   колбасá   b   помидóры   c   рýсские закýски

Now how would you say you don't like them?

4   Unscramble the following dialogue by numbering the phrases 1 to 5.

Хорошó. Дáйте мне, пожáлуйста, торт.
Торт с фрýктами. Это óчень вкýсно.
Слýшаю вас.
Молодóй человéк!
Что вы рекомендýете на десéрт?

now you're **talking!**

1 **2•71** Imagine you're at the **ресторáн Москóвский** for a meal.

- ♦ Call the waiter and ask for the menu.
- ● **Вот меню.**
- ♦ Thank him.
- ● **Пожáлуйста.**

2 **2•72** He returns a few minutes later to take your order.

- ● **Слýшаю вас.**
- ♦ Ask for sardines in oil.
- ● **А на пéрвое?**
- ♦ Order beetroot soup.
- ● **Хорошó, а на вторóе?**
- ♦ Say you like fish and ask what he recommends.
- ● **Сегóдня есть карп с грибáми. Это óчень вкýсно.**
- ♦ Order the carp with mushrooms.
- ● **Что вы бýдете пить?**
- ♦ Ask him to give you a white wine.

3 **2•73** He comes back while you're eating your main meal.

- ● **Всё нормáльно? Вам нрáвится карп?**
- ♦ Tell him that you like it very much.
- ● **Что вы бýдете на десéрт?**
- ♦ Say *nothing* and explain that you don't like dessert.

quiz

1 What would you be given if you asked for the **меню**?

2 If you want to call the waiter, would you say:

   a **Де́вушка!** or b **Молодо́й челове́к!** ?

3 Put the following dishes in the order you normally eat them:

   a **второ́е**   b **сла́дкое**   c **пе́рвое**   d **заку́ски**

4 If the waitress says: **Слу́шаю вас,** what should you do?

5 What drink do you associate with a **самова́р**?

6 To say you like **блины́** would you use:

   a **мне нра́вится** or b **мне нра́вятся**?

7 Which is the odd one out?

   a **мя́со**   b **ры́ба**   c **квас**   d **колбаса́**

Now check whether you can …

- understand the main points of a Russian menu
- ask what dishes are available
- order a meal with drinks
- say what you like and what you don't like

Бра́во! *Well done!* You have reached the end of Talk Russian.
Now prepare yourself for **Контро́льная рабо́та 3** *Checkpoint 3* with
some revision. Listen to the conversations again – the more you listen
the more confident you will become. You can test your knowledge
of the key phrases by covering up the English on the lists. Look back
at the final pages of each unit and use the quizzes and checklists to
assess how much you remember.

Take every opportunity to speak Russian; if no one else is available,
talk out loud to yourself.

Контро́льная рабо́та 3

1 2•74 In the **спра́вочное бюро́** at the **вокза́л** you hear people asking about train times. Listen and match the train numbers to the correct times.

a по́езд но́мер 13 **b** по́езд но́мер 6
c по́езд но́мер 20 **d** по́езд но́мер 8

| 10:10 | 07:30 | 21:15 | 23:50 |

2 You need a drink, so you ask someone where the snack-bar is. Which of these questions would you ask?

a Скажи́те, пожа́луйста, где гости́ница?
b Скажи́те, пожа́луйста, здесь есть буфе́т?
c Скажи́те, пожа́луйста, здесь есть магази́н?

3 The person you ask replies **Вот нале́во – буфе́т.**
Should you turn to your left or your right?

4 In the **буфе́т** you look at the drinks available.
a Tick all the cold, non-alcoholic drinks.
b How would you ask for a tea with lemon?

Напитки

вино́	ко́фе	пи́во
ви́ски	лимона́д	тома́тный сок
во́дка	минера́льная вода́	фа́нта
квас	молоко́	чай
конья́к	пе́пси-ко́ла	шампа́нское

5   **2•75** The man standing next to you looks very friendly, so you decide to try out your Russian. Check your answers with the audio.

    a   Greet him and tell him you're English.
    b   Ask him if he's Russian and where he lives.
    c   Tell him you like Moscow very much.

6   **2•76** You then ask him where the **Гости́ница Пра́га** is. Listen and write down in English the directions he gives you.

    ....

    ....

    ....

7   You've found the **Гости́ница Пра́га**. At reception you are waiting behind a woman who says she's booked a double room with a shower. Which of the following do you hear her say?

    a   **Я заказа́л одноме́стный но́мер с ду́шем.**
    b   **Я заказа́л одноме́стный но́мер с ва́нной.**
    c   **Я заказа́ла двухме́стный но́мер с ду́шем.**
    d   **Я заказа́ла но́мер люкс.**

8   The receptionist tells her that her room is:

на четвёртом этажé

What floor would she be on?

9 While you're waiting at reception, you see lots of Russian signs. Look at the following and say what they mean.

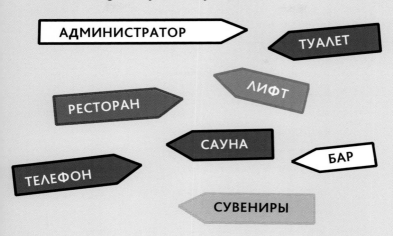

АДМИНИСТРАТОР

ТУАЛЕТ

ЛИФТ

РЕСТОРАН

САУНА

БАР

ТЕЛЕФОН

СУВЕНИРЫ

10 2•77 Now it's your turn to check in. You'll need to know how to:

- say that you've booked a single room with a bath for three days
- ask if you can dine in the hotel
- check which floor the restaurant is on
- make sure that you can pay by credit card

11 2•78 Later, you dine in the hotel restaurant, very keen to try **традицио́нная ру́сская ку́хня**. Listen to the audio. You'll need to know how to ask for the following:

- mushrooms in sour cream
- clear soup with pasties
- lamb kebabs
- pancakes with jam
- a Russian soft drink made from black bread and yeast

12 After your meal you go to the **бар** for a drink. You pick up a children's magazine, **Весёлые Картинки** (literally *Jolly Pictures*), and see the following quiz page. You have to match a word from the left column with one from the right. Try it!

1	рубль	дом
2	бассе́йн	чек
3	бар	музе́й
4	ма́рка	закры́т
5	кварти́ра	вода́
6	ка́сса	банк
7	Эрмита́ж	кафе́
8	откры́т	откры́тка

13 Now try the word search before going up to your **но́мер**.

апте́ка	ко́фе	спаси́бо
до свида́ния	откры́то	у́лица
здра́вствуйте	по́чта	центр
кафе́	рестора́н	что

а	н	ц	у	е	т	й	у	в	т	с	в	а	р	д	з	а
я	к	а	е	н	г	ш	щ	л	з	х	ф	ы	в	а	п	р
и	о	л	р	д	б	э	я	ч	и	с	м	и	т	б	ю	ж
н	ь	ь	ё	о	ц	р	т	н	е	ц	у	к	е	н	г	ш
а	а	в	ы	ф	т	д	л	о	р	п	а	п	т	е	к	а
д	н	с	ч	я	э	с	у	в	т	с	в	о	р	д	з	а
и	т	и	м	с	п	й	е	т	б	о	т	ч	ю	ё	й	ц
в	е	к	у	а	т	й	у	р	т	с	в	т	р	е	н	г
с	н	а	с	е	е	ф	о	к	л	о	р	а	л	д	э	ж
о	т	и	а	м	и	т	р	в	а	х	щ	г	п	т	о	я
д	б	а	ф	е	т	ы	щ	э	ы	ф	т	м	н	у	я	г
о	в	п	х	д	т	й	и	л	ю	щ	е	о	м	ш	а	е
в	ё	п	х	о	т	ы	у	р	н	э	д	к	и	л	х	ш

Transcripts and answers

This section contains scripts of all the conversations. Answers which consist of words and phrases from the conversations are given in bold type in the scripts. Other answers are given separately.

Unit 1

Pages 8 & 9 Saying hello, goodbye and how are you

2 ● **Здра́вствуйте.**
  ◆ Здра́вствуйте.

3 ● Здра́вствуйте.
  ◆ Здра́вствуйте.
  ● **Здра́вствуй.**
  ◆ Здра́вствуйте.
  ● **Здра́вствуй.**

There are 2 young people/children.

4 ● Здра́вствуйте. *(1 hello)*
  ◆ Здра́вствуйте. *(2 hello)*
  ● До свида́ния. *(3 goodbye)*
  ◆ Здра́вствуйте. *(4 hello)*
  ● До свида́ния. *(5 goodbye)*

6 ● Здра́вствуйте. Как у вас дела́?
  ◆ Спаси́бо, хорошо́. А как у вас?
  ● Спаси́бо, хорошо́.

How are you?

7 ● Как дела́?
  ◆ Спаси́бо, хорошо́.

Fine, thank you.

8 *1* До свида́ния.
  2 А как у вас?
  3 Здра́вствуйте.
  4 Спаси́бо, хорошо́.
  5 Как у вас дела́?
  6 Здра́вствуй.

Pages 10 & 11 Introducing yourself and asking someone's name

2 ● Здра́вствуйте. Меня́ зову́т Óльга.

  ◆ Меня́ зову́т Ива́н.
  ● Меня́ зову́т Та́ня.
  ◆ А меня́ зову́т Ви́ктор.

Olga, Ivan, Tanya, Victor.

4 ● Здра́вствуйте. Как вас зову́т?
  ◆ Меня́ зову́т Ви́ктор.
  ● **Прости́те?**
  ◆ Меня́ зову́т Ви́ктор.
  ● **Óчень ра́да.**
  ◆ Óчень рад.

She says Óчень ра́да *because a woman says 'pleased to meet you' in a different way from a man.*

5 Anna   Здра́вствуйте.
  Tanya *(b)* **Здра́вствуйте.**
  Anna   Как *(d)* **вас** зову́т?
  Tanya Меня́ зову́т Та́ня.
          (a) **Как** вас зову́т?
  Anna   *(e)* **Меня́** зову́т Áнна,
          а как тебя́ зову́т?
  Boris Меня́ зову́т Бори́с.
  Anna   Óчень ра́да.
  Boris *(c)* **Óчень** рад.

6 *1* Меня́ зову́т Áнна.
  2 Как вас зову́т?
  3 Óчень рад.
  4 Как тебя́ зову́т?
  5 Прости́те?
  6 Как дела́?

Page 12 Put it all together

2 *a* but/and; *b* how; *c* mum; *d* tact;
  e atom; *f* coma; *g* attack; *h* comet

3 *a* underground/metro; *b* theatre;
  c restaurant; *d* tractor; *e* course;
  f Moscow; *g* orchestra; *h* character

4 *a* Goodbye; *b* What's your name?;
  c My name's Anna; *d* Pleased to meet you; *e* How are you?

Page 13 Now you're talking!

1 ● **Здра́вствуйте.**
  ◆ Здра́вствуйте. Как у вас дела́?

- **Спаси́бо, хорошо́. А как у вас?**
- ◆ Спаси́бо, хорошо́.

- **Здра́вствуйте. Меня́ зову́т +
  your name.**
- ◆ О́чень рад. Меня́ зову́т Ива́н.
- **Прости́те?**
- ◆ Меня́ зову́т Ива́н.
- **До свида́ния.**

2 • **Здра́вствуйте.**
- ◆ Здра́вствуйте.
- **Здра́вствуй.**
- ◆ Здра́вствуйте.
- **Как тебя́ зову́т?**
- ◆ Меня́ зову́т Са́ша.
- **Как дела́?**
- ◆ Спаси́бо, хорошо́.

3 • **Здра́вствуйте.**
- **Как вас зову́т?**
- **Как у вас дела́?**
- **До свида́ния.**

Page 14 Quiz

1 c; *2* Moscow; *3* His mum; *4* In a
restaurant; *5* b; *6* very well; *7* a; *8* b;
9 b; *10* a.

Unit 2

Pages 16 & 17 Asking someone's
nationality and stating yours

2 • Дави́д, вы америка́нец?
- ◆ Нет, я не америка́нец. Я кана́дец.
- Анн, а вы америка́нка?
- ◆ Да, я америка́нка.
- Ли́са, вы америка́нка?
- ◆ Нет, я англича́нка.
- Марк, а вы англича́нин?
- ◆ Нет, я не англича́нин. Я
  австрали́ец.

*David is Canadian; Ann is American; Lisa is
English; Mark is Australian.*

3 *a* America; *b* Canada; *c* England;
d Russia; *e* Britain; *f* Australia

4 *1*d; *2*c; *3*b; *4*a; *5*f; *6*e
2 and 4 are women.

5 *a* Englishman; *b* American woman;
c Russian man; *d* Canadian man

Page 18 Saying whether you are
married

2 • Дави́д, вы жена́ты?
- ◆ Да, я жена́т.
- Анн, вы за́мужем?
- ◆ Нет, я не за́мужем.
- Ли́са, вы за́мужем?
- ◆ Да, я за́мужем.
- Марк, вы жена́ты?
- ◆ Нет, я не жена́т.

David and Lisa are married.

3 • Меня́ зову́т О́льга Ива́новна.
  Я ру́сская. Я москви́чка. Я не
  за́мужем.

b and c are true

4 • Меня́ зову́т Анн. Я америка́нка. Я
  не за́мужем.
- ◆ Меня́ зову́т Ли́са. Я англича́нка. Я
  за́мужем.
- Меня́ зову́т Дави́д. Я кана́дец. Я
  жена́т.
- ◆ Меня́ зову́т Марк. Я австрали́ец.
  Я не жена́т.

*Ann – American – unmarried; Lisa – English
– married; David – Canadian – married;
Mark – Australian – unmarried.*

Page 19 Using the numbers 0 to 4

2 *a* 2; *b* 4; *c* 3; *d* 1; *e* 0

3 *a* 2; *b* 3; *c* 1; *d* 4

4 *1* Она́ не америка́нка.
  2 Вы англича́нин?
  3 Вы жена́ты?
  4 Да, он англича́нин.
  5 Она́ за́мужем.
  6 Вы за́мужем?
  7 Она́ москви́чка.
  8 Ты жена́т?

Page 20 Put it all together

2 *a* gas; *b* newspaper; *c* gesture;
  d taxi

3 *a* litre; *b* match (sport);
c you (formal); *d* I

4 *a* whisky; *b* kilogram(me);
c Chekhov; *d* kiosk; *e* toilet;
f wine; *g* a Muscovite (m);
h a Muscovite (f)

5 *a* She's married; *b* He's married;
c She's a student; *d* He's a student;
e I'm not English (m)

Page 21 Now you're talking!

1 ● **Здра́вствуйте.**
   ◆ Здра́вствуйте. Как вас зову́т?
   ● **Меня́ зову́т Мари́я Фо́стер. Как
     вас зову́т?**
   ◆ Меня́ зову́т Ива́н. Как у вас дела́?
   ● **Спаси́бо, хорошо́. Вы москви́ч?**
   ◆ Да, я москви́ч.
   ● **Я англича́нка.**
   ◆ О́чень рад.
   ● **О́чень ра́да.**

2 ● **Меня́ зову́т Росс Смарт.**
   ◆ Я студе́нт.
   ● Я америка́нец.
   ◆ Я жена́т.

3 ● **Вы ру́сский?**
   ◆ **Вы москви́ч?**
   ● **Вы студе́нт?**
   ◆ **Вы жена́ты?**

Page 22 Quiz

1 b; *2* Britain; *3* b d a c; *4* Canada;
5 a Yes b No; *6* c; *7* b; *8* Moscow; *9* Anna;
10 Chekhov.

Unit 3

Pages 24 & 25 Introducing friends and members of your family

2 Olga   Это моя́ подру́га *(a)* **Ле́на.**
                (Lyena)
    David О́чень рад.
    Olga   Это мой друг *(b)* **Лев.** *(Lyev)*
    David О́чень рад.

3 ● Это мой муж **Ви́ктор.** *(Victor)*
   ◆ Это моя́ жена́ **Ли́дия.** *(Lydia)*

5 ● Ле́на, у вас есть де́ти?
   ◆ Да, у меня́ есть сын.
   ● Лев, у вас есть сын?
   ◆ Нет, у меня́ есть дочь.
   a Да *b* Нет.

6 ● Это моя́ подру́га.
   ◆ Как её зову́т?
   ● Её зову́т **Ни́на.** *(Nina)*
   ◆ О́чень рад.
   ● О́чень ра́да.
   ◆ А это мой друг.
   ● Как его́ зову́т?
   ◆ Его́ зову́т **Па́вел.** *(Pavel)*

Page 26 Talking about your family

2 ● Ни́на, у вас есть брат?
   ◆ Да, два.
   ● Па́вел, у вас есть сестра́?
   ◆ Да, её зову́т Со́ня.
   ● У вас есть де́ти?
   ◆ Нет, я не жена́т.
   c and d are true

3 Меня́ зову́т Ве́ра. Я за́мужем. Это
   мой *(b)* **муж.** Его́ зову́т Серге́й.
   У меня́ есть сын. Его́ зову́т *(e)*
   Никола́й. Он не *(f)* **жена́т.** У меня́
   та́кже есть *(d)* **дочь.** Её зову́т Ири́на.
   Она́ *(a)* **за́мужем.** У неё есть дочь,
   ита́к я *(c)* **ба́бушка.**

Page 27 Giving your phone number

2 *a* 6; *b* 8; *c* 10; *d* 9; *e* 7; *f* 5.

3 Меня́ зову́т Дави́д. Мой но́мер
   телефо́на **1670521** *(David)*

   Меня́ зову́т Марк. Мой но́мер
   телефо́на **9324186** *(Mark)*

5 *1* У вас есть де́ти?
   2 Это мой муж.
   3 Это твой брат?
   4 Это моя́ подру́га.
   5 У неё есть сын.
   6 Как его́ зову́т?

Page 28 Put it all together

2 *a* bar; *b* lady; *c* her; *d* my; *e* park;
f examination

3 car

4 *a* diploma; *b* bus; *c* Tolstoy;
d expert; *e* university; *f* tram

5 *a* This is Victor; *b* Is this your wife?
c I also have a son; *d* He has a son;
e What's her name? *f* Have you any
children?

Page 29 Now you're talking!

1 ● **Я женат.**
  ◆ Это ваша жена?
  ● **Да, её зовут Рита.**
  ◆ У вас есть дети?
  ● **Да у меня есть сын. Его зовут
    Грег.**
  ◆ Он женат?
  ● **Он не женат. У него есть дочь.**
  ◆ А …, хорошо.

2 ● **Меня зовут Лиса Паркер.**
  ● **Я студентка.**
  ● **Я англичанка.**
  ● **Я замужем.**
  ● **У меня есть дочь.**
  ● **Её зовут Ванесса.**

Page 30 Quiz

1 b; *2* informal; *3* e c a d f b; *4* your phone
number; *5* b; *6* Tolstoy; *7* also; *8* female

Unit 4

Pages 32 & 33 Ordering a drink in a
bar or cafe

2 ● Что вам угодно?
  ◆ Кофе, пожалуйста.
coffee

3 ● Что вам угодно?
  ◆ Пиво, пожалуйста.
  ● Вино, пожалуйста.
  ◆ Лимонад, пожалуйста.
  ● Вода, пожалуйста.

  ◆ Пиво, вино, лимонад и вода?
    Хорошо.
папа: пиво (dad: beer); мама: вино
(mum: wine); сын: лимонад (son:
lemonade); дочь: вода (daughter: water)

4 ● Чай, пожалуйста.
  ◆ Кофе, пожалуйста.
  ● С сахаром?
  ◆ Нет, спасибо, без сахара.
*The man has tea; the woman has coffee
without sugar.*

5 ● Кофе, пожалуйста, с молоком без
    сахара.
a, with milk, no sugar

6 ● Чай с лимоном, пожалуйста.
lemon

7 ● Минеральная вода, пожалуйста.
  ◆ С газом или без газа?
  ● Без газа, пожалуйста.
still mineral water

8 ● **Пиво, пожалуйста.**
  ◆ **Кофе с молоком, пожалуйста.**
  ● **Чай без сахара, пожалуйста.**

Page 34 Offering, accepting or
refusing a drink

2 ● Что вы хотите?
  ◆ Пепси-кола, пожалуйста.
  ● Пепси-кола? Хорошо.
  ◆ Спасибо.
  ● **Пожалуйста** *(b)*
He asks for a coke.

3 ● **Что ты хочешь** *(b)*, Катя?
  ◆ Сок, пожалуйста.
  ● А ты, Миша, что хочешь?
  ◆ Коньяк, пожалуйста.
Misha orders cognac/brandy; Anna uses
Что ты хочешь? *as she knows Katya
well.*

Page 35 Using the numbers 11 to 20

2 ● Лимонад. Двенадцать,
    пожалуйста. *12*
  ◆ Пепси-кола. Одиннадцать,

пожа́луйста. *11*
- Моро́женое. Пятна́дцать, пожа́луйста. *15*

3 *a 16; b 13; c 20; d 14; e 19*

4 *1* Что ты хо́чешь? *2* Конья́к, пожа́луйста. *3* Конья́к? Хорошо́. *4* Спаси́бо. *5* Пожа́луйста.

Page 36 Put it all together

2 *a* Fanta/fizzy orange; *b* centre; *c* champagne; *d* beetroot soup; *e* menu

3 object

4 *a* administrator; *b* telephone; *c* concert; *d* Tchaikovsky; *e* Russia; *f* St Petersburg.

5 *a* A beer, please; *b* What would you like? *c* Tea with milk; *d* Coffee without sugar; *e* You're welcome.

Page 37 Now you're talking!

1 • **Что ты хо́чешь?**
- ◆ Пи́во, пожа́луйста.
- **Что вы хоти́те?**
- ◆ Пе́пси-ко́ла, пожа́луйста.
- **Здра́вствуйте. Пи́во, пе́пси-ко́ла и лимона́д, пожа́луйста.**

2 • **Здра́вствуйте.**
- ◆ Здра́вствуйте. Что вам уго́дно?
- **Чай, пожа́луйста.**
- ◆ С са́харом?
- **С са́харом без молока́.**
- ◆ Хорошо́.
- **Спаси́бо.**
- ◆ Пожа́луйста.

3 • **И́горь, ты хо́чешь ко́фе?**
- ◆ С са́харом?
- **С молоко́м?**
- ◆ **Ко́фе с молоко́м без са́хара, пожа́луйста.**

Page 38 Quiz

1 a; *2* brandy; *3* b a c; *4* coffee, a coffee, the coffee; *5* n; *6* lemon; *7* ice cream; *8* still; *9* barman

Контро́льная рабо́та 1
Pages 39–42

1 • Здра́вствуйте. Как вас зову́т?
- ◆ Меня́ зову́т **Ро́бин Мо́рсон**.
- Вы англича́нин?
- ◆ Нет, **я австрали́ец**.
- Вы жена́ты?
- ◆ Да, **я жена́т**.
- У вас есть де́ти?
- ◆ Да, **у меня́ есть сын**.
- Как его́ зову́т?
- ◆ **Его́ зову́т Кри́стофер**.

Ро́бин Мо́рсон австрали́ец. Он жена́т. У него́ есть сын. Его́ зову́т Кри́стофер.

2 • Дави́д, Э́то моя́ ма́ма.
- ◆ О́чень ра́да.
- ◆ О́чень рад.
- А э́то моя́ сестра́. Её зову́т Зи́на.
- Здра́вствуй, Зи́на. Как дела́?
- Спаси́бо, хорошо́. Вы англича́нин?
- Нет, я кана́дец.

David meets Anton's mum and sister; Anton's sister's name is Zina; she says she is well; David is from Canada.

3 • Что ты хо́чешь, Дави́д? Есть вино́, пи́во, чай и́ли ко́фе.

c лимона́д.

4 *vodka; brandy; fizzy orange; tea; tomato juice; lemonade; wine; gin; coffee; champagne; whisky; rum; milk; water; coke.*

5 *Ireland; Wales; Scotland; Italy; Spain; France; Greece; Bulgaria; Germany*

6 *1* h; *2* g; *3* a; *4* f; *5* b; *6* d; *7* e; *8* c

7 *a* 29; *b* 19; *c* 25; *d* 31; *e* 31

8 *1* e; *2* d; *3* a; *4* f; *5* b; *6* c

9 *1* c **a**нглича́нин; *2* d **м**еня́; *3* f **Е**ё; *4* e **р**ад; *5* a **И**ва́н; *6* g **К**ак; *7* b **a**мерика́нка

The country is Аме́рика.

10 Dear Elizabeth. My name's Masha. I'm a Muscovite. I'm a student in Moscow. My dad's an engineer

and my mum's a guide. I have
a sister. Her name's Natasha.
She's a schoolgirl. I also have a
grandmother. My phone number
is 007 095 1670355. Goodbye.
Masha.

Unit 5
Pages 44 & 45 Asking where something is and how far it is

2 • Прости́те, пожа́луйста, где
   по́чта?
   ♦ Иди́те нале́во.
   • Скажи́те, пожа́луйста, где
   метро́?
   ♦ Иди́те пря́мо.
   • Скажи́те, пожа́луйста, где теа́тр?
   ♦ Иди́те пря́мо.
   • Прости́те, пожа́луйста, где
   гости́ница?
   ♦ Иди́те напра́во.
   • Скажи́те, пожа́луйста, где
   рестора́н?
   ♦ Иди́те пря́мо.
   • Скажи́те, пожа́луйста, где музе́й?
   ♦ Иди́те нале́во.

a post office, left; *b* underground,
straight on; *c* theatre, straight on;
d hotel, right; *e* restaurant, straight on;
f museum, left

4 • Теа́тр? Э́то далеко́?
   ♦ Да, далеко́, два́дцать мину́т
   авто́бусом.
   • Музе́й – далеко́?
   ♦ Пять мину́т пешко́м.
   • А по́чта? Э́то далеко́?
   ♦ Нет, недалеко́, две мину́ты
   пешко́м.
   • Гости́ница – далеко́?
   ♦ Пятна́дцать мину́т авто́бусом.
   • Рестора́н – далеко́?
   ♦ Де́сять мину́т авто́бусом.
   • А метро́ – далеко́?
   ♦ Нет, оди́н киломе́тр, двена́дцать
   мину́т пешко́м.
   • Оди́н киломе́тр!! Э́то далеко́!

a 20 by bus; *b* 5 on foot; *c* 2 on foot; *d* 15
by bus; *e* 10 by bus; *f* 12 on foot

Page 46 Asking where someone lives

2 • Ли́са, где вы живёте?
   ♦ Я живу́ в Ло́ндоне.
   • Дави́д, где вы живёте?
   ♦ Я живу́ в Ванку́вере.
   • Марк, где вы живёте?
   ♦ Я живу́ в Канбе́рре.
   • Анн, где вы живёте?
   ♦ Я живу́ в Нью-Йо́рке.

*Lisa lives in London; David lives in
Vancouver; Mark lives in Canberra; Ann
lives in New York.*

3 • **Лев**, ты живёшь в Москве́?
   ♦ Нет, я живу́ в Волгогра́де.
   • Пётр, вы живёте в Москве́?
   ♦ Нет, я живу́ в Но́вгороде.

*Лев lives in Volgograd and is the one Olga
knows well. Пётр lives in Novgorod.*

Page 47 Using the numbers 21 to 199

2 • Я живу́ в до́ме трина́дцать, в
   кварти́ре во́семьдесят де́вять.
a д. 13 кв. 89
   ♦ Я живу́ в до́ме три́дцать четы́ре,
   в кварти́ре пятьдеся́т три.
b д. 34 кв. 53
   • Я живу́ в до́ме два́дцать два, в
   кварти́ре сто се́мьдесят во́семь.
c д. 22 кв. 178
   ♦ Я живу́ в до́ме со́рок шесть, в
   кварти́ре сто девяно́сто семь.
d д. 46 кв. 197

Page 48 Put it all together

1 *a* right; *b* left; *c* straight on

2 *a* 35 kilometres; *b* 51 minutes;
   c 48 minutes; *d* 92 minutes;
   e 61 kilometres; *f* 83 kilometres

3 *a* Петербу́рг; *b* со́рок; *c* метро́;
   d пря́мо

4 *1* c; *2* a; *3* d; *4* b

Page 49 Now you're talking!

1 ● **Скажи́те, пожа́луйста, где метро́?**
 ◆ Метро́? Иди́те нале́во.
 ● **Э́то далеко́?**
 ◆ Нет, пять мину́т пешко́м.
 ● **Где по́чта?**
 ◆ По́чта? Иди́те пря́мо.
 ● **Спаси́бо.**

2 ● Вы ру́сский?
 ◆ **Нет, я америка́нец. Вы ру́сский?**
 ● Да, я ру́сский.
 ◆ **Вы живёте в Санкт-Петербу́рге?**
 ● Да. Где вы живёте?
 ◆ **Я живу́ в Нью-Йо́рке**
 ● А ..., хорошо́.
 ◆ **Скажи́те, пожа́луйста, где Эрмита́ж?**
 ● Эрмита́ж? Иди́те нале́во и пря́мо.
 ◆ **Э́то далеко́?**
 ● Нет, де́сять мину́т пешко́м.
 ◆ **Спаси́бо. До свида́ния.**

Page 50 Quiz
1 right; *2* b; *3* a; *4* a (the/a) theatre (singular), b (the) theatres (plural); *5* b; *6* in a flat; *7* c

Unit 6
Pages 52 & 53 Understanding what there is in town and when it's open

2 банк *bank*; библиоте́ка *library*; апте́ка *chemist's*; кино́ *cinema*; буфе́т *snackbar*; галере́я *gallery*; магази́н *shop*; универма́г *department store*; суперма́ркет *supermarket*; бассе́йн *swimming pool*; парк *park*; ры́нок *market*

3 ● Здесь есть **магази́ны**?
 ◆ Да, здесь есть **универма́г** и **суперма́ркет**.
 ● Где здесь **банк**?
 ◆ Здесь нет ба́нка. Вот план го́рода. Банк в це́нтре.

There is a bank in the centre.

5 *a* Э́то **откры́то** в суббо́ту. *Saturday.*
 b Э́то **откры́то** в четве́рг. *Thursday.*
 c Э́то **закры́то** в воскресе́нье. *Sunday.*

Pages 54 & 55 Making simple enquiries and asking for help to understand

2 ● Скажи́те, пожа́луйста, здесь есть туале́т?
 ◆ Да, здесь нале́во.
 ● Спаси́бо. А здесь есть телефо́н?
 ◆ Нет, здесь нет телефо́на.
a да; *b* нет; *c* да

3 ● Скажи́те, пожа́луйста, где здесь по́чта?
 ◆ Прости́те, **я не зна́ю** (с). Я не москви́ч.

4 ● Скажи́те, пожа́луйста, где здесь по́чта?
 ◆ По́чта? Иди́те пря́мо, пото́м напра́во.
 ● Она́ откры́та?
 ◆ Да, сего́дня откры́та.
Straight on, then right.
She wants to get to the post office. It's open.

6 David (d) **Скажи́те, пожа́луйста, где здесь библиоте́ка?**
 Passer-by В це́нтре, на у́лице Че́хова.
 David Прости́те, я не понима́ю. Повтори́те пожа́луйста.
 Passer-by Библиоте́ка в (f) **це́нтре**, на у́лице Че́хова.
 David Спаси́бо. Она́ откры́та во вто́рник?
 Passer-by Да, она́ (a) **откры́та**.
 David А здесь есть банк?
 Passer-by Есть.
 David Он откры́т?
 Passer-by Нет, сего́дня (g) **закры́т**.
 David Говори́те, пожа́луйста, (e) **ме́дленно**.
 Passer-by (b) **Сего́дня** банк закры́т.

David Спаси́бо.
Passer-by *(c)* **Пожа́луйста.**

Page 56 Put it all together

1 *a* Monday; *b* Tuesday to Friday;
c 12.00 to 18.00; *d* Sunday

Page 57 Now you're talking!

1 ● **Скажи́те, пожа́луйста, здесь
есть универма́г?**
   ◆ Да, есть, на у́лице Пу́шкина.
   ● **Я не понима́ю. Повтори́те,
пожа́луйста.**
   ◆ Да, есть, на у́лице Пу́шкина.
   ● **Универма́г откры́т?**
   ◆ Да, он откры́т.
   ● **Спаси́бо. Здесь есть апте́ка?**
   ◆ Апте́ка? Иди́те напра́во, пото́м
пря́мо.
   ● **Говори́те, пожа́луйста,
ме́дленно.**
   ◆ Апте́ка – напра́во, пото́м пря́мо.
   ● **Напра́во, пото́м пря́мо. Она́
откры́та?**
   ◆ Да, она́ откры́та.
   ● **Спаси́бо.**
   ◆ Пожа́луйста.

2 ● **Вот план го́рода.**
   ◆ **Магази́ны в це́нтре.**
   ● **Здесь есть ры́нок в четве́рг.**
   ◆ **По́чта закры́та в воскресе́нье.**
   ● **Здесь нет ба́нка.**

Page 58 Quiz

1 in the centre; *2* closed; *3* a map of the
town; *4* b; *5* c a b; *6* Sunday; *7* a

Unit 7

Pages 60 & 61 Using the numbers
above 200 and understanding prices

2 *a* 5р 22к; *b* 41р 15к; *c* 1 363р

3 *a* 7р 60к; *b* 107р 50к; *c* 1 196р 75к

5 откры́тка *postcard*; почто́вая ма́рка
postage stamp; аспири́н *aspirin*;
фотоаппара́т *camera*; шампа́нское
champagne; сувени́ры *souvenirs*

6 ● Ско́лько сто́ит **аспири́н?** *(aspirin)*
   ◆ **Сто пятьдеся́т рубле́й.**
(150 roubles)

7 ● Здра́вствуйте. У вас есть
фотоаппара́т?
   ◆ Да, вот фотоаппара́ты.
   ● Ско́лько сто́ят?
   ◆ **Шесть ты́сяч две́сти два́дцать
пять рубле́й.**
(6225 roubles)
   ● Спаси́бо. Да́йте, пожа́луйста,
оди́н. Скажи́те, пожа́луйста,
ско́лько сто́ит **шампа́нское?**
   ◆ **Восемьсо́т рубле́й.**
(800 roubles)
*шампа́нское 800 roubles;
фотоаппара́т 6225 roubles*

8 ● Здра́вствуйте. Ско́лько сто́ят
откры́тки?
   ◆ **Три́дцать рубле́й.**
(30 roubles)
   ● Да́йте, пожа́луйста, **три.**
(3). Ско́лько сто́ит **ма́рка в
Аме́рику?**
   ◆ **Два́дцать три рубля́.**
(23 roubles)
*postcard costs 30 roubles; she buys 3;
stamp for America costs 23 roubles*

Pages 62 & 63 Asking for items in a
shop or market

2 ● Здра́вствуйте. У вас есть
сувени́ры?
   ◆ Да. Что вы хоти́те?
   ● Я не зна́ю.
   ◆ Вот матрёшка и́ли ша́пка.
   ● Мо́жно посмотре́ть?
   ◆ Мо́жно. Вот, пожа́луйста.
   ● Ско́лько сто́ит ша́пка?
   ◆ Две ты́сячи рубле́й.
   ● Хорошо́. А ско́лько сто́ит
матрёшка?
   ◆ Семьсо́т рубле́й. Вы хоти́те?
   ● Да, пожа́луйста.
   ◆ Э́то всё?
   ● Да, э́то всё.
   ◆ Плати́те в ка́ссу.

set of Russian dolls

3 • Матрёшка, **семьсо́т рубле́й**.
 ◆ Вот **чек** и сда́ча.
 • Спаси́бо.
 ◆ Пожа́луйста.
700 roubles; a receipt

4 У вас есть ло́жки? Мо́жно
 посмотре́ть?
 У вас есть во́дка? Мо́жно
 посмотре́ть?
 У вас есть икра́? Мо́жно
 посмотре́ть?
 У вас есть матрёшка? Мо́жно
 посмотре́ть?
 У вас есть ша́пка? Мо́жно
 посмотре́ть?

5 *a* (bread); *b* (apples); *c* (tomatoes);
 d (cheese); *e* (milk)

6 • Ско́лько сто́ят **я́блоки**?
 ◆ Шестьдеся́т рубле́й килогра́мм.
 • Да́йте мне, пожа́луйста,
 килогра́мм.
 ◆ Что ещё?
 • **Помидо́ры** – полкило́,
 пожа́луйста.
 ◆ Э́то всё?
 • Да, э́то всё.
 ◆ Со́рок рубле́й.
 • Спаси́бо.
 ◆ Пожа́луйста.

 • **Молоко́**, пожа́луйста, – паке́т.
 ◆ Что ещё?
 • **Сыр**, пожа́луйста, – две́сти
 пятьдеся́т грамм.
 ◆ Что ещё?
 • Э́то всё, спаси́бо.
1 b я́блоки; *2 c* помидо́ры; *3 e* молоко́;
4 d сыр.
She forgets to buy bread – a хлеб.

Page 64 Put it all together

1 *a* 1 917; *b* 7 496; *c* 22 583; *d* 500 155

2 *a* May I have a look? *b* Could you give
 me …? *c* That's all; *d* How much is it?
 e Have you got …? *f* Anything else?
 g How much are they?

3 *1* У вас есть помидо́ры? *2* Да, есть.
 3 Ско́лько сто́ят? *4* пятьдеся́т
 рубле́й – килогра́мм. *5* Да́йте,
 пожа́луйста, полкило́.

4 150g cheese; 2 loaves; 4 tomatoes;
 1 litre mineral water; half kg apples

Page 65 Now you're talking!

1 • **Здра́вствуйте. У вас есть
 сувени́ры?**
 ◆ Да. Что вы хоти́те?
 • **Я не зна́ю.**
 ◆ Вот, пожа́луйста, ло́жки и́ли
 матрёшка.
 • **Мо́жно посмотре́ть?**
 ◆ Мо́жно. Вот, пожа́луйста.
 • **Ско́лько сто́ят ло́жки?**
 ◆ Две́сти рубле́й.
 • **(А) ско́лько сто́ит матрёшка?**
 ◆ Семьсо́т рубле́й.
 • **Да́йте, пожа́луйста, ло́жки.**
 ◆ Хорошо́. Э́то всё?
 • **Да, э́то всё, спаси́бо.**
 ◆ Плати́те в ка́ссу две́сти рубле́й.

2 • **Ло́жки. Две́сти рубле́й**.
 ◆ Пожа́луйста, чек.
 • **Спаси́бо.**
 ◆ Пожа́луйста.

3 • **Пожа́луйста, чек** or **Вот чек**.
 ◆ Пожа́луйста, ло́жки.
 • **Спаси́бо.**
 ◆ Пожа́луйста.

Page 66 Quiz

1 b; *2* b; *3* 100; *4* a large department
store in Moscow; *5* to pay at the cash
desk; *6* b; *7* c

Контро́льная рабо́та 2
Pages 67–70

1 • Прости́те, пожа́луйста, здесь
 есть **банк**?
 ◆ Иди́те пря́мо. Э́то у́лица Го́голя.
 Вот нале́во – банк.
 • Спаси́бо.
 ◆ Пожа́луйста.
a bank (box 1)

- Скажи́те, пожа́луйста, где **рестора́н** Кали́нка?
- Иди́те пря́мо, напра́во, пото́м нале́во. Э́то у́лица Сре́тенка. Вот напра́во – рестора́н Кали́нка.
- Повтори́те, пожа́луйста.
- Иди́те пря́мо, напра́во, пото́м нале́во. Э́то у́лица Сре́тенка. Вот напра́во – рестора́н Кали́нка.

b Kalinka restaurant (*box 3*)

- Скажи́те, пожа́луйста, где здесь **по́чта**?
- По́чта? Иди́те пря́мо, пото́м напра́во. Э́то Проспе́кт Ми́ра. Вот напра́во – по́чта.
- Прости́те, я не понима́ю. Говори́те, пожа́луйста, ме́дленно.
- А ..., хорошо́. Иди́те пря́мо, пото́м напра́во. Э́то Проспе́кт Ми́ра. Вот напра́во – по́чта.

c post office (*box 2*)

2
- Прости́те, пожа́луйста, банк откры́т?
- Нет, сего́дня **закры́т**.

a closed

- Скажи́те, пожа́луйста, рестора́н Кали́нка откры́т?
- Да, он **откры́т**.

b open

- Скажи́те, пожа́луйста, по́чта откры́та?
- Да, она́ **откры́та**.

c open

3
во́дка – литр	**240**р.
молоко́ – паке́т	**48**р.
хлеб – бато́н	**36**р.
сыр – 300г	**100**р.
помидо́ры – полкило́	**20**р.

4 a Moscow; b 52; c Ivanov

5 a суббо́та; b чек; c кварти́ра; d ша́пка

6 1 b; 2 e; 3 c; 4 a; 5 d

7 1 b; 2 a; 3 e; 4 c; 5 d

8 a нет; b да; c нет; d да; e да; f нет; g да

Unit 8

Page 72 Checking in at reception

2
- Здра́вствуйте. Меня́ зову́т Бен Бра́ун. Я заказа́л **двухме́стный но́мер с ду́шем**.
- Ваш па́спорт, пожа́луйста.
- Вот мой па́спорт.

double room with a shower

- Здра́вствуйте. Я заказа́ла **одноме́стный но́мер с ду́шем**.
- Ва́ша фами́лия, пожа́луйста.
- Смит.

single room with a shower

- Здра́вствуйте.
- Здра́вствуйте. Я заказа́ла **но́мер лю́кс**.
- Ва́ша фами́лия, пожа́луйста.
- А́ндерсон.
- А́ндерсон. Вот ... но́мер три́ста пять **с ва́нной и с ду́шем**.

luxury room with a bath and shower

Page 73 Asking if there's a room free

2
- Здра́вствуйте. У вас есть свобо́дный но́мер?
- На ско́лько челове́к?
- На **два**.
- На ско́лько дней?
- На **три дня**.
- Како́й но́мер вы хоти́те?
- Но́мер **с ва́нной**, пожа́луйста.
- Ва́ша фами́лия, пожа́луйста.
- **Каре́нин**.

фами́лия: Каре́нин; коли́чество челове́к: два; коли́чество дней: три дня; но́мер: с ва́нной

- Здра́вствуйте. У вас есть свобо́дный но́мер?
- Како́й но́мер вы хоти́те?
- **С ду́шем**, пожа́луйста.
- На ско́лько дней?

- На **семь дней**.
- И на ско́лько челове́к?
- На **два**.
- Хорошо́. Ва́ша фами́лия, пожа́луйста.
- **Петро́ва**.
- Ваш па́спорт, пожа́луйста.
- Вот мой па́спорт.

фами́лия: Петро́ва; коли́чество челове́к: два; коли́чество дней: семь дней; но́мер: с ду́шем

Page 74 Asking which floor something is on

2 *a* 7th; *b* 11th; *c* 5th; *d* 8th

3
- Ва́ша фами́лия, пожа́луйста.
- **Бра́ун**.
- Ваш но́мер **на оди́ннадцатом этаже́**.

- Ва́ша фами́лия, пожа́луйста.
- **Смит**.
- Вы **на седьмо́м этаже́**.

- Ва́ша фами́лия, пожа́луйста.
- **А́ндерсон**.
- Но́мер три́дцать, **на пе́рвом этаже́**.

1 b; *2* a; *3* c

Page 75 Making requests

2
- Мо́жно оплати́ть креди́тной ка́ртой?
- Мо́жно.
- Мо́жно заказа́ть такси́?
- Стоя́нка такси́ нале́во, недалеко́.

a By credit card; *b* On the left, not far.

- Мо́жно посмотре́ть но́мер?
- Да, он на второ́м этаже́.
- Где лифт?
- Здесь, напра́во.

c 1st (literally 2nd in English); *d* On the right.

- Мо́жно пообе́дать в гости́нице?
- Да, рестора́н откры́т.

e Yes.

Page 76 Put it all together

1 *1* У вас есть свобо́дный но́мер?
   2 Да, есть. На ско́лько дней?
   3 На три дня.
   4 И на ско́лько челове́к?
   5 На два.
   6 Есть двухме́стный но́мер на седьмо́м этаже́.
   7 Мо́жно посмотре́ть но́мер?
   8 Мо́жно. Вот ключ.

2 *1* d; *2* a; *3* b; *4* c; *5* e

3 *1* b; *2* e; *3* a; *4* d; *5* c

Page 77 Now you're talking!

1
- **Здра́вствуйте. У вас есть свобо́дный но́мер?**
- Одноме́стный и́ли двухме́стный но́мер?
- **Одноме́стный с ду́шем, пожа́луйста.**
- На ско́лько дней?
- **На два дня.**
- Хорошо́. Есть свобо́дный но́мер на пя́том этаже́.
- **Мо́жно посмотре́ть?**
- Мо́жно. Вот ключ.

2
- Ва́ша фами́лия, пожа́луйста.
- **Петро́ва**.
- Ваш па́спорт, пожа́луйста.
- **Вот мой па́спорт.**
- Спаси́бо.
- **Мо́жно пообе́дать в гости́нице?**
- Да, рестора́н откры́т.
- **Рестора́н на како́м этаже́?**
- На тре́тьем этаже́.
- **Мо́жно оплати́ть креди́тной ка́ртой?**
- Да, мо́жно.
- **Спаси́бо.**
- Пожа́луйста.

Page 78 Quiz

1 a; *2* passport; *3* ground floor; *4* manager; *5* registration form; *6* lift; *7* surname.

Unit 9

Page 80 Asking about public transport

2 • Скажи́те, пожа́луйста, како́й
  трамва́й идёт до **метро́**?
  ◆ Трамва́й но́мер **се́мьдесят три.**
a tram; 73; the Metro (underground)

  • Прости́те, пожа́луйста, како́й
    тролле́йбус идёт до
    по́чты?
  ◆ **Тролле́йбус** но́мер **три.**
b trolleybus; 3; post office

  • Скажи́те, пожа́луйста, есть
    автобус до **Эрмита́жа**?
  ◆ Есть. Автобус но́мер **два́дцать
    четы́ре.** Иди́те напра́во, там
    остано́вка.
c bus; 24; the Hermitage (museum)

3 **Есть автобус до аэропо́рта?
  Како́й тролле́йбус идёт до
  вокза́ла?
  Како́й трамва́й идёт до у́лицы
  Пу́шкина?**

Page 81 Finding out train times

2 *a* 21.15; *b* 17.21; *c* 22.43; *d* 06.35

3 • Скажи́те, пожа́луйста, когда́
    отхо́дит по́езд до Оде́ссы?
  ◆ В **03.00.**
  • А когда́ я бу́ду в Оде́ссе?
  ◆ В **23.30.**
depart 03.00; arrive 23.30

  • Когда́ отхо́дит сле́дующий по́езд
    до Я́лты?
  ◆ В **02.50.**
  • А в кото́ром часу́ я бу́ду в Я́лте?
  ◆ В **22.45.**
depart 02.50; arrive 22.45

  • Прости́те, пожа́луйста, в кото́ром
    часу́ отхо́дит сле́дующий по́езд
    до Ки́ева?
  ◆ В **08.05.**

  • А когда́ я бу́ду в Ки́еве?
  ◆ В **21.58.**
depart 08.05; arrive 21.58

Page 82 Buying train tickets

2 • Оди́н биле́т до Москвы́,
    пожа́луйста.
  ◆ В оди́н коне́ц и́ли туда́ и
    обра́тно?
  • **В оди́н коне́ц**, пожа́луйста.

  ◆ Да́йте мне, пожа́луйста, два
    биле́та до Но́вгорода.
  • В оди́н коне́ц и́ли туда́ и
    обра́тно?
  ◆ **В оди́н коне́ц**, пожа́луйста.
  • Пожа́луйста, три ты́сячи две́сти
    де́сять рубле́й.

  ◆ Да́йте мне, пожа́луйста, биле́т до
    Оде́ссы.
  • Биле́т в оди́н коне́ц?
  ◆ Нет, **биле́т туда́ и обра́тно**,
    пожа́луйста.

  • Да́йте, пожа́луйста, **биле́т в
    оди́н коне́ц** до Со́чи.
  ◆ две ты́сячи восемьсо́т рубле́й.

3 • Прости́те, пожа́луйста, с како́й
    платфо́рмы отхо́дит по́езд до
    Но́вгорода?
  ◆ С платфо́рмы но́мер **три.**
a Novgorod; platform 3

  • Скажи́те, пожа́луйста, с како́й
    платфо́рмы отхо́дит сле́дующий
    по́езд до **Я́лты**?
  ◆ С платфо́рмы но́мер
    оди́ннадцать.
b Yalta; platform 11

  • Прости́те, пожа́луйста, с како́й
    платфо́рмы отхо́дит по́езд до
    Москвы́?
  ◆ С платфо́рмы но́мер **четы́ре.**
c Moscow; platform 4

  • С како́й платфо́рмы отхо́дит

следующий поезд до **Одессы**?
- ◆ С платфо́рмы но́мер **семь**.

d Odessa; platform 7

Page 83 Finding your way around the Metro

2 ● Прости́те, где мо́жно купи́ть биле́т на метро́?
- ◆ На́до купи́ть биле́т в ка́ссе. Иди́те напра́во, там ка́сса.

● Скажи́те, пожа́луйста, где ста́нция Ки́евская?
- ◆ Вот схе́ма метро́ и вот – Ки́евская.

● Спаси́бо. На́до де́лать переса́дку?
- ◆ Нет, не на́до.

● Скажи́те мне, пожа́луйста, когда́ на́до выходи́ть?
- ◆ Сле́дующая ста́нция Ки́евская.

a Нет; *b* Нет; *c* Да.

3 ● 1 Ста́нция **Пло́щадь Револю́ции** … Осторо́жно, две́ри закрыва́ются. Сле́дующая ста́нция Арба́тская.

● 2 Ста́нция **Арба́тская** … Осторо́жно, две́ри закрыва́ются. Сле́дующая ста́нция Смоле́нская.

● 3 Ста́нция **Смоле́нская** . . . Осторо́жно, две́ри закрыва́ются. Сле́дующая ста́нция Ки́евская.

● 4 Ста́нция **Ки́евская** . . . Осторо́жно, две́ри закрыва́ются. Сле́дующая ста́нция Парк Побе́ды.

Page 84 Put it all together

1 *1* c; *2* e; *3* a; *4* d; *5* b

2 *a* в час; *b* в трина́дцать часо́в; *c* в четы́ре часа́; *d* в шестна́дцать часо́в; *e* в семь часо́в де́сять мину́т;

f в девятна́дцать часо́в де́сять мину́т.

3 *1* d; *2* e; *3* b; *4* a; *5* c

4 *a* авто́бус; *b* по́езд; *c* тролле́йбус; *d* трамва́й

Page 85 Now you're talking!

1 ● **Э́то далеко́?**
- ◆ Нет, де́сять мину́т тролле́йбусом.

● **Како́й тролле́йбус?**
- ◆ Тролле́йбус но́мер два́дцать шесть.

● **Где остано́вка?**
- ◆ Иди́те нале́во, там остано́вка.

2 ● **Скажи́те, пожа́луйста, где ста́нция Ки́евская?**
- ◆ Вот схе́ма метро́ и вот – Ки́евская.

● **На́до де́лать переса́дку?**
- ◆ Нет, не на́до.

3 ● **Биле́т в оди́н коне́ц до Санкт-Петербу́рга, пожа́луйста.**
- ◆ Две ты́сячи шестьсо́т рубле́й.

● **Когда́ отхо́дит сле́дующий по́езд?**
- ◆ В два́дцать два часа́.

● **С како́й платфо́рмы отхо́дит по́езд?**
- ◆ С платфо́рмы но́мер двена́дцать.

Page 86 Quiz

1 aeroplane; *2* for information; *3 a* railway station *b* Metro station; *4* b; *5* return; *6* change trains; *7* c; *8* a

Unit 10

Page 90 Asking what's available

2 ● Молодо́й челове́к! Да́йте, пожа́луйста, **меню́**.
- ◆ Пожа́луйста, меню́.

the menu

3 ● Каки́е заку́ски у вас есть?
- ◆ Есть **колбаса́**, **винегре́т**, **грибы́ в смета́не**, **сарди́ны в ма́сле**.

- У вас есть **чёрная икра́**?
- Нет, то́лько **кра́сная икра́**.

1 d; *2* f; *3* e; *4* c; *5* b; *6* a
There is no black caviar – b чёрная икра́.

4
- А что у вас есть сего́дня на пе́рвое?
- Пожа́луйста, есть щи, борщ и бульо́н.
- У вас есть **уха́**?
- Есть.

fish soup

5
- Сего́дня на второ́е есть шашлы́к, бефстро́ганов, ку́рица с ри́сом, карп с гриба́ми.

a да; *b* нет; *c* нет; *d* да

Page 91 Ordering a meal

2
- Де́вушка!
- Слу́шаю вас.
- Да́йте, пожа́луйста, **винегре́т**.
- Хорошо́. А вы хоти́те суп?
- Спаси́бо, нет. Что вы рекоменду́ете на второ́е?
- **Ку́рицу с ри́сом**.
- Да́йте мне, пожа́луйста, ку́рицу.
- А на десе́рт?
- **Моро́женое**, пожа́луйста.

3
- Что вы бу́дете пить?
- **Во́дку**, пожа́луйста.

vodka

4
- Де́вушка! Счёт, пожа́луйста.
- **Одна́ ты́сяча семьсо́т пятьдеся́т рубле́й**.

c 1750 рубле́й.

Pages 92 & 93 Saying what you like and don't like

2
- Мне нра́вится **ры́ба**. Тебе́ нра́вится карп, Ми́ша?
- Да, мне нра́вится **карп**.
- Что тебе́ нра́вится, Пётр?
- Мне нра́вится **бефстро́ганов**.
- А Ната́ша …?
- Мне нра́вится **бифште́кс**.

a ма́ма; *b* дочь (Ната́ша); *c* сын (Пётр); *d* па́па (Ми́ша)

3
- Мне нра́вится икра́.
- Мне нра́вятся блины́.
- Мне нра́вится кра́сное вино́.
- Мне нра́вится холо́дные заку́ски.

5
- Слу́шаю вас.
- Да́йте, пожа́луйста, **грибы́ в смета́не**. Мне о́чень нра́вятся.
- Хорошо́.

mushrooms in sour cream

6
- Да́йте мне, пожа́луйста, **сала́т**.
- Пётр, что ты хо́чешь?
- Икру́, пожа́луйста.
- Тебе́ бо́льше нра́вится кра́сная и́ли **чёрная икра́**?
- Чёрная, коне́чно.

7
- Ната́ша, что ты хо́чешь?
- Спаси́бо, ничего́. Мне не нра́вятся холо́дные заку́ски.

She doesn't like cold starters.

8

Метрдоте́ль	*(b)* **Всё** норма́льно?
Па́па	*(d)* **Да**, спаси́бо.
Метрдоте́ль	Тебе́ *(a)* **нра́вится** десе́рт?
Пётр	Да, э́то о́чень *(c)* **вку́сно**.

Page 94 Put it all together

1 *a* with jam; *b* in tomato sauce; *c* fried; *d* in butter; *e* garnished with vegetables; *f* with mushrooms; *g* tasty

2 заку́ски – *d* икра́, *j* винегре́т
пе́рвые блю́да – *g* борщ, *i* щи
вторы́е блю́да – *b* шашлы́к
c ку́рица *e* щу́ка
десе́рт – *a* торт *f* я́блоки
h моро́женое

3 *a* **Мне нра́вится колбаса́.**
b **Мне нра́вятся помидо́ры.**
c **Мне нра́вятся ру́сские заку́ски.**

To say you don't like them, add **не** *after* **Мне**.

4 *1* Молодо́й челове́к! *2* Слу́шаю вас.
3 Что вы рекоменду́ете на десе́рт?
4 Торт с фру́ктами. Э́то о́чень

вкусно. 5 Хорошо. Дайте мне, пожалуйста, торт.

Page 95 Now you're talking!

1 • **Молодой человек! Дайте, пожалуйста, меню.**
  ◆ Вот меню.
  • **Спасибо.**
  ◆ Пожалуйста.

2 • Слушаю вас.
  ◆ **Сардины в масле, пожалуйста.**
  • А на первое?
  ◆ **Борщ, пожалуйста.**
  • Хорошо, а на второе?
  ◆ **Мне нравится рыба. Что вы рекомендуете?**
  • Сегодня есть карп с грибами. Это очень вкусно.
  ◆ **Карп с грибами, пожалуйста.**
  • Что вы будете пить?
  ◆ **Дайте мне пожалуйста, белое вино.**

3 • Всё нормально? Вам нравится карп?
  ◆ **Мне очень нравится.**
  • Что вы будете на десерт?
  ◆ **Спасибо, ничего. Мне не нравится десерт.**

Page 96 Quiz

1 menu; *2* b; *3* d c a b; *4* give your order; *5* tea (чай); *6* b; *7* c

Контрольная работа 3
Pages 97–100

1 • Когда отходит поезд номер тринадцать?
  ◆ **В семь часов тридцать минут.**
  a 07.30

  • В котором часу отходит поезд номер шесть?
  ◆ **В двадцать три часа пятьдесят минут.**
  b 23.50

  • В котором часу отходит следующий поезд до Минска?

  ◆ Поезд номер двадцать отходит **в десять часов десять минут.**
  c 10.10.

  • Когда отходит поезд до Волгограда?
  ◆ Поезд номер восемь отходит **в двадцать один час пятнадцать минут.**
  d 21.15.

2 *b* Скажите, пожалуйста, здесь есть буфет?

3 *left*

4 *a* квас; лимонад; минеральная вода; молоко; пепси-кола; томатный сок; фанта

  b чай с лимоном.

5 *a* **Здравствуйте. Я англичанин (m)/англичанка (f).**
  b **Вы русский? Где вы живёте?**
  c **Мне очень нравится Москва.**

6 • Скажите, пожалуйста, где гостиница Прага?
  ◆ Гостиница Прага? Идите направо. Это улица Дурова. Идите прямо, потом налево. Это Манежная площадь и вот налево – гостиница Прага.

Go right. This is Durova Street. Go straight on, then left. This is Manezhnaya Square and the Hotel Prague is to your left.

7 *c* Я заказала двухместный номер с душем.

8 *3rd floor*

9 АДМИНИСТРАТОР *manager*; ТУАЛЕТ *toilet*; РЕСТОРАН *restaurant*; ЛИФТ *lift*; ТЕЛЕФОН *telephone*; САУНА *sauna*; БАР *bar*; СУВЕНИРЫ *souvenirs*

10 **Я заказал(а) одноместный номер с ванной на три дня. Можно пообедать в гостинице? Ресторан на каком этаже? Можно оплатить кредитной картой?**

11 Дайте мне, пожалуйста:
грибы в сметане
бульон с пирожками
шашлык
блины с вареньем
квас

12 1 рубль/банк
2 бассейн/вода
3 бар/кафе
4 марка/открытка
5 квартира/дом
6 касса/чек
7 Эрмитаж/музей
8 открыт/закрыт

13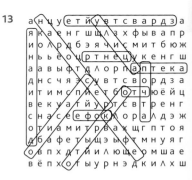

pronunciation

The Russian alphabet is on page 6.

Once you know how the letters and combinations of letters are pronounced and how they function in words, you'll know how to pronounce any Russian word you come across. There's no choice as with, for example, the English *a*, which can be *cat*, *care*, *war*, *woman*; or *ough*, which can be *cough*, *through*, *though*, *thought*.

stress

As in English, one syllable of every Russian word is stressed, i.e. emphasised, more than the others. In this book stress is marked by the sign ´ over the vowel. And as in English, the position of the stress affects pronunciation, e.g. *the Sahara désert* and the verb *to desért*. Stress in Russian is more unpredictable, shifting even within the same word depending on whether it's singular or plural, or what grammatical case it is.

- **Ë** is always stressed, so no stress sign is needed: **тётя** *aunt*.
- **O** is pronounced differently depending on whether it is stressed or not.

  бюро́ *office*, stressed **o** is pronounced like the *o* in *hot* but with more rounded lips: *byuro*

  Бори́ос *Boris*, **o** before the stressed syllable sounds like *a*: *Ba̲rees*

  го́род *town*, **o** after the stressed syllable sounds like *er* in *mother*: *goru̲d*.

hard and soft sounds

Most Russian consonants have a hard and a soft sound, depending on what comes after them. The tongue is nearer to the roof of the mouth when pronouncing soft consonants, and there's a hint of an English *y* sound. A consonant is soft if it is followed by the vowels **е ё и ю я** or the soft sign **ь**. It's useful to think of Russian as having five pairs of vowels, which make consonants hard or soft:

hard		soft	
а	*a* as in *cat*	**я**	*ya* as in **ya**k
э	*e* as in **e**gg	**е**	*ye* as in **ye**t
ы	*i* as in *big*	**и**	*ee* as in *feed*
о	*o* as in *hot*	**ё**	*yo* as in **yo**gurt
у	*oo* as in *mood*	**ю**	*yoo*

Of the consonants, three are always hard no matter which letter follows them: **ж ц** and **ш**. Two are always soft as the *y* sound is already within their pronunciation: **ч** and **щ**. The letter **й** is, strictly speaking, a consonant, although it is a special case. It almost always appears after a vowel to form a single, extended sound or diphthong, similar to the effect of *y* in the English words *day* and *boy*: **Алексéй** *Aleksei*, **Толстóй** *Tolstoi*. It can begin foreign words to represent the sound *y*: **йóгурт** *yogurt*, **Нью-Йóрк** *New York*. It is treated as soft when it comes to choosing endings (see page 121).

hard	soft
Лóндон *London* pronounced *Lonn-dann* with hard *L* as in the English *lot* because it's followed by the vowel **о**.	**Лéнин** *Lenin* pronounced *Lyenin* with soft *L* because it's followed by the vowel **е**.
буфéт *buffet* pronounced *boofyet* with hard *b* as in the English *boot* because it's followed by the vowel **у**.	**бюрó** *office* pronounced *byuro* with soft *b* as in the English *beauty* because it's followed by the vowel **ю**.
лимóн *lemon* pronounced *leemon* with hard *n* as in the English *noodle* because it is not followed by **ь** or a vowel.	**день** *day* pronounced *dyen(y)* with soft *n*, pronounced a little like *ny* in the English *news* because it's followed by the soft sign **ь**.
брат *brother* pronounced *brat* with hard *t* as in the English *top* because it's not followed by the soft sign **ь** or a vowel.	**есть** *there is/are* pronounced *yest(y)* with soft *t*, pronounced *ty* as in the Russian name *Katya* because it's followed by the soft sign **ь**.
центр *centre* pronounced *tsentr*, not *tsyentr*, because **ц** is always hard.	**щи** *cabbage soup* pronounced *shchyee*, not *shchi*, as **щ** is always soft.

Being able to distinguish whether a word ends in a hard or soft sound will help with choosing which set of endings to use when forming the various cases (see page 121).

grammar

Grammar explains how a language works. When you're learning a new language it really helps to learn some basic rules, which are easier to follow if you understand these essential grammatical terms.

Nouns are the words for living beings, things, places and abstract concepts: *daughter*, *designer*, *Rachel*, *shark*, *hat*, *village*, *Moscow*, *measles*, *freedom*.

Gender: in Russian every noun is masculine (m), feminine (f) or neuter (n). This is its gender, and you need to know a noun's gender because words used with it, such as adjectives, have corresponding masculine, feminine and neuter forms.

Number refers to **singular**, meaning one, or **plural**, meaning more than one.

Pronouns are words used to avoid repeating the noun: *I, me, we, us, you, he/she, him/her, it, they, them, this/those, mine/yours*.

Adjectives are words that describe nouns and pronouns: <u>*good*</u> *idea*; <u>*strong red*</u> *wine*; *she's* <u>*tall*</u>; *those are* <u>*odd*</u>. When a Russian adjective is used with a noun, it has to agree with, i.e. match, that noun in terms of gender, number and case.

Prepositions are words like *in*, *at*, *to*, *opposite*, *beside*, *from*, *over*, *before*, which are usually followed by a noun.

Verbs are words like *go*, *sleep*, *eat*, *like*, *have*, *be*, *live*, *die*, that relate to doing and being. In English, they can have *to* before them: *to go*, *to sleep*, this is called the **infinitive**.

The **subject** of a sentence is the person/thing carrying out the action: <u>*the man*</u> *saw the children*.

The **object** of a sentence is at the receiving end of the action. It can be **direct**: *the man saw* <u>*the children*</u>, or **indirect**: *the man spoke* <u>*to the children*</u>.

A **negative** sentence uses *not* with the verb.

The **endings** of words are the final letter(s). In English, a verb ending in -*ed* tells you it happened in the past, and a noun with an added -**s** indicates a plural. Endings are much more widespread in Russian; nouns, adjectives and verbs rely on them to convey essential information.

Case refers to the role of a noun, pronoun or adjective in a sentence: whether they're the subject or the object, or whether they follow a particular preposition. They have a different ending for each of the different cases.

nouns

Every Russian noun is one of three genders: masculine (m), feminine (f) or neuter (n). With few exceptions, you can tell the gender of a noun from its ending:

masculine	Most masculine nouns end in a consonant (including **й**), or soft sign. A few end in **а** or **я**; these always refer to a male person: **лимона́д** *lemonade*, **душ** *shower* **чай** *tea*, **трамва́й** *tram* **рубль** *rouble*, **день** *day* **мужчи́на** *man*, **дя́дя** *uncle*
feminine	Feminine nouns end in **а**, **я** or a soft sign: **газе́та** *newspaper*, **икра́** *caviar* **ку́хня** *kitchen*, **А́нглия** *England* **пло́щадь** *square*, **дверь** *door*
neuter	Neuter nouns end in **о** or **е**: **вино́** *wine*, **ма́сло** *butter/oil* **варе́нье** *jam*, **по́ле** *field*

Nouns ending in the soft sign **ь** can be either masculine or feminine. There's no logic to this and so the gender has to be learnt:

рубль (m) *rouble*, **день** (m) *day*, **пло́щадь** (f) *square*, **дверь** (f) *door*

> Russian has no words for *a*, *the* or *some*: **лимона́д** means *lemonade*, *a lemonade*, *the lemonade* or *some lemonade*. The meaning is understood from the context.

case

Case is an important element of Russian grammar. Words have different endings in a sentence according to whether they're the subject or the object of the verb, whether they have another function, or whether they follow a particular preposition. These are known as **case endings** and they affect nouns, adjectives and pronouns. There are six grammatical cases in Russian:

nominative: the form found in a dictionary, used for the subject of a sentence. It is also used after **есть** *there is/are*; *have*.

<u>Дом</u> на у́лице Че́хова. <u>*The house*</u> *is on Chekhov Street.*
<u>По́езд</u> отхо́дит в семь часо́в. <u>*The train*</u> *leaves at seven o'clock.*
Здесь есть <u>банк</u>? *Is there <u>a bank</u> here?*; У меня́ есть <u>сын</u>. *I have <u>a son</u>.*

accusative: used for the direct object of a sentence.

Я рекоменду́ю ку́рицу. *I recommend the chicken.*

Да́йте я́блоко. *Give (me) an apple.*

genitive: used to mean *of* or to show possession, like *'s* in English.

Дом Ната́ши. *Natasha's house.*

Да́йте план го́рода. *Give me a map of the town.*

The genitive is also used:
- after **нет** *there isn't a (any)/there aren't any*
  Нет Лимона́да. *There isn't any lemonade.*
  Нет газе́ты. *There isn't a newspaper.*
- after all numbers that don't end with a 1 (page 128)
  Два ключа́ *two keys;* **Три дня** *three days;* **Два́дцать пять рубле́й** *twenty-five roubles*

dative: used for the indirect object of the sentence.

Да́йте биле́т Алексе́ю. *Give the ticket to Aleksei.*

Скажи́те Та́не. *Tell Tanya.*

instrumental: used to express *by* or *by means of*.

Пять мину́т авто́бусом. *Five minutes by bus.*

Мо́жно оплати́ть креди́тной ка́ртой? *May I pay by credit card?*

prepositional: used with a preposition to express location.

Я живу́ в Москве́. *I live in Moscow.*

Музе́й на у́лице Че́хова. *The museum is on Chekhov Street.*

case endings: nouns

All of these endings look daunting when set out in tables, but don't worry – you will find that individual words tend to be used most often in just one or two cases, and practice will help you remember them. For instance, the instrumental case translates the English *by*, so it is commonly seen on nouns denoting transport e.g. **авто́бусом** *by bus;* **трамва́ем** *by train.* The numbers *two* upwards are followed by the genitive singular or plural, so words relating to money and time are commonly seen in the genitive: **два рубля́** *two roubles;* **де́сять мину́т** *ten minutes.*

Case endings in Russian are affected by whether the noun is considered to be 'hard' or 'soft' (see page 117).

- Nouns ending in a consonant (except **й**), **а**, or **о** are hard and take the hard set of endings in other cases.
- Nouns ending in **я**, **е**, **й** or the soft sign **ь** are soft and take the soft set of endings in other cases.

singular

	m (hard) -**д**	m (soft) -**й**	m (soft) -**ь**
nominative	лимона́**д**	ча**й**	рубл**ь**
accusative	лимона́**д**	ча**й**	рубл**ь**
genitive	лимона́**да**	ча́**я**	рубл**я́**
dative	лимона́**ду**	ча́**ю**	рубл**ю́**
instrumental	лимона́**дом**	ча́**ем**	рубл**ём**
prepositional	лемона́**де**	ча́**е**	рубл**е́**

	f (hard) -**а**	f (soft) -**я**	f (soft) -**ь**
nominative	газе́т**а**	ку́хн**я**	пло́щад**ь**
accusative	газе́т**у**	ку́хн**ю**	пло́щад**ь**
genitive	газе́т**ы**	ку́хн**и**	пло́щад**и**
dative	газе́т**е**	ку́хн**е**	пло́щад**и**
instrumental	газе́т**ой**	ку́хн**ей**	пло́щад**ью**
prepositional	газе́т**е**	ку́хн**е**	пло́щад**и**

	n (hard) -**о́**	n (soft) -**е**
nominative	вин**о́**	по́л**е**
accusative	вин**о́**	по́л**е**
genitive	вин**а́**	по́л**я**
dative	вин**у́**	по́л**ю**
instrumental	вин**о́м**	по́л**ем**
prepositional	вин**е́**	по́л**е**

Spelling rule 1: The consonants **г к х ч ш щ** and **ж** cannot be followed by **ы**. Instead you write **и**. This affects feminine nouns in the genitive singular and nominative and accusative plural: **подру́га** *female friend* → **подру́ги**; **ша́пка** *cap* → **ша́пки**, and masculine nouns in the nominative and accusative plural: **банк** *bank* → **ба́нки** *banks*; **ключ** *key* → **ключи́** *keys*.

It also affects adjectives (see pages 124–125) – masculine adjectives in the nominative, accusative and instrumental singular, neuter instrumental singular, and all plurals: **ру́сский го́род** *a Russian town*; **с хоро́шим дру́гом** *with a Russian friend*; **горя́чие пирожки́** *hot pies*; **с ру́сскими блина́ми** *with Russian pancakes*

Spelling rule 2: the consonants **ч ш щ ж** and **ц** cannot be followed by an unstressed **о**. Instead you write **е**. This affects nouns in the instrumental case:
ключ *key* → **ключо́м** (followed by a stressed **о**)
душ *shower* → **ду́шем** (unstressed ending)
гости́ница *hotel* → **гости́ницей** (unstressed ending)
It also affects adjectives of all genders in most cases:
Нет горя́чей воды́ *There's no hot water* (genitive); **хоро́шее вино́** *good wine* (nominative, accusative)

Exceptions
- Masculine nouns ending in **a** or **я** take the same endings as feminine nouns ending in these letters.
- Some masculine nouns lose their final vowel in all cases apart from the nominative singular: **день** *day* → **дня, дню** etc; **ры́нок** *market* → **ры́нка, ры́нку** etc.
- The prepositional of feminine nouns ending in **ия** is **ии**: **А́нглия** → **(в) А́нглии** *(in) England*; **Австра́лия** → **(в) Австра́лии** *(in) Australia*
- The prepositional of some short masculine nouns ends in **у**, which is always stressed: **час** *hour* **(в)** → **часу́**; **год** *year* → **(в) году́**

Some neuter nouns don't change at all – in any grammatical case. These are almost always words borrowed from other languages, and include **бюро́** *office*, **кафе́** *cafe*, **метро́** *metro*, **кино́** *cinema*.

plural
There is more similarity between the genders in the plural endings, with the genitive case being the only tricky one.

- Nouns ending in a consonant except **й** (masculine), **a** (feminine), or **о** (neuter) take the hard set of endings.
- Nouns ending in **й** (masculine), the soft sign **ь** (masculine or feminine), **я** (feminine), or **е** (neuter), take the soft set of endings.

	hard	soft
nominative	**-ы** (m and f); **-а** (n)	**-и** (m and f); **-я** (n)
accusative	**-ы** (m and f); **-а** (n)	**-и** (m and f); **-я** (n)
genitive	*see below	*see below
dative	**-ам**	**-ям**
instrumental	**-ами**	**-ями**
prepositional	**-ах**	**-ях**

Где гости́ницы? *Where are the hotels?*
суп с гриба́ми *mushroom soup* (lit. *soup with mushrooms*)

Exceptions

- A few masculine nouns in the nominative/accusative plural have the stressed ending **á**: **го́род** *town* → **города́**; **дом** *house* → **дома́** *houses*.
- The nominative/accusative plural of **я́блоко** (n) *apple* is **я́блоки**.

*genitive plurals

masculine
Nouns ending in a consonant add **ов**: **лимона́д** *lemonade* → **лимона́дов**
Nouns ending in **й** replace this with **ев** (or **ёв** if stressed): **чай** *tea* → **чаёв**
Nouns ending in a soft sign **ь** replace this with **ей**: **рубль** *rouble* → **рубле́й**

feminine
Nouns ending in **а** drop this: **газе́та** *newspaper* → **газе́т**. A vowel may be added to ease pronunciation: **откры́тка** *postcard* → **откры́ток**
Nouns ending in **я** replace this with **ь**; a vowel may be added to ease pronunciation: **ку́хня** *kitchen*→ **ку́хонь**
Nouns ending in a soft sign **ь** replace this with **ей**: **пло́щадь** *square* → **площаде́й**

neuter
Nouns ending in **о** drop this: **вино́** *wine* → **вин**
Nouns ending in **е** change this to **ей**: **по́ле** *field* → **поле́й**

adjectives

Adjectives are either hard or soft, and this is indicated by their ending: **кра́сный** *red* is hard and **си́ний** *blue* is soft. The endings of adjectives are formed of two letters, and it is the first of the two (i.e. the penultimate letter of the word) that indicates whether the adjective is hard or soft.

Adjectives have to agree with, i.e. match, what they describe in terms of gender, number and case.

Masculine adjectives have the endings: **ый** (standard hard ending where the stress is on the stem, not the ending), **ой** (stressed hard ending), **ий** (soft ending).

тома́тный сок *tomato juice*; кра́сный трамва́й *red tram*; выходно́й день *day off*; си́ний дом *blue house*

Feminine adjectives have the endings: **ая** (hard), **яя** (soft):
кра́сная икра́ *red caviar*; си́няя ва́за *blue vase*

Neuter adjectives have the endings: **ое** (hard), **ее** (soft):
кра́сное вино́ *white wine*; си́нее море *the blue sea*

singular

	m hard	m hard	f hard	n hard
nominative	кра́сный	выходно́й	кра́сная	кра́сное
accusative	кра́сный	выходно́й	кра́сную	кра́сное
genitive	*кра́сного	*выходно́го	кра́сной	*кра́сного
dative	кра́сному	выходно́му	кра́сной	кра́сному
instrumental	кра́сным	выходны́м	кра́сной	кра́сным
prepositional	кра́сном	выходно́м	кра́сной	кра́сном

	m soft	f soft	n soft
nominative	си́ний	си́няя	си́нее
accusative	си́ний	си́нюю	си́нее
genitive	*си́него	си́ней	*си́него
dative	си́нему	си́ней	си́нему
instrumental	си́ним	си́ней	си́ним
prepositional	си́нем	си́ней	си́нем

*The **г** of **ого** and **его** is pronounced *v*, not *g*.

Я рекоменду́ю кра́сную икру́. *I recommend the red caviar.*
буты́лка кра́сного вина́ *bottle of red wine*
оплати́ть креди́тной ка́ртой *to pay with a credit card*
В кото́ром часу́? *At what time* (lit. *hour*)?

plural

There are only two sets of endings for adjectives in the plural, one hard and one soft. They are used for all genders.

	hard	soft
nominative	-ые	-ие
accusative	-ые	-ие
genitive	-ых	-их
dative	-ым	-им
instrumental	-ыми	-ими
prepositional	-ых	-их

национа́льные блю́да *national dishes* (nominative, accusative)
килогра́мм кра́сных помидо́ров *a kilogram of red tomatoes* (genitive)
в си́них ва́зах *in (the) blue vases* (prepositional)

pronouns

The subject personal pronouns in the nominative case are:

я	*I*	мы	*we*
ты	*you*	вы	*you*
он	*he/it*	они́	*they*
она́	*she/it*		
оно́	*it*		

There are two words for *you* in Russian:

ты someone you call by their first name: a friend, member of the family, young person

вы (often written **Вы**) someone you don't know well, someone older, more than one person

personal pronouns change according to gender, case and number. The accusative, genitive and dative forms of the personal pronouns are:

nominative	accusative	genitive	dative
я	меня́	меня́	мне
ты	тебя́	тебя́	тебе́
он, оно́	его́*	его́*	ему́
она́	её**	её**	ей
мы	нас	нас	нам
вы	вас	вас	вам
они́	их*	их*	им

*The **г** of **его** is pronounced *v*, not *g*.

word begins with an **н when following a preposition:

У неё есть ... *She has ...*

accusative

Меня зовут ... *My name is ...* (lit. *They call me ...*)

Как вас/тебя зовут? *What's your (formal/informal) name?*

genitive

У меня/вас есть ... *I/you have ...* (lit. *In the possession of me there is*)

У него есть/У них есть ... *He has/they have ...*

dative

Мне нравится/тебе нравится ... *I/you like ...* (lit. *... likes itself to me*)

Дайте мне ... *Give (to) me ...*

possessives

English has possessive adjectives *my*, *your*, *our*, etc. and possessive pronouns *mine*, *yours*, *ours* etc. Russian uses the same words for both.

	m	f	n	pl
my/mine	мой	моя	моё	мои
your, yours **ты**	твой	твоя	твоё	твои
his, its	его*			
her, hers, its	её			
our, ours	наш	наша	наше	наши
your, yours **вы**	ваш	ваша	ваше	ваши
their, theirs	их			

*The **г** of **его** is pronounced *v*, not *g*.

мой билет *my ticket*; **твой билет** *your ticket*

мои дети *my children*; **твои дети** *your children*

Лимонад мой/твой. *The lemonade is mine/yours.*

ключи ваши? *Are the keys yours?*

Нет, ключи наши. *No, the keys are ours.*

prepositions

Nouns/pronouns following Russian prepositions are in specific cases.

* **в** *to/at/on* + days of week, **на** *for* + **accusative**
  Платите в кассу. *Pay at the cash desk.*
  в субботу *on Saturday*
  Что вы будете на десерт? *What do you want for dessert?*

- **с** *from*, **До** *to/up to/as far as*, **без** *without*, **у** *in the possession* + **genitive**
  По́езд отхо́дит с платфо́рмы … *The train leaves from platform …*
  По́езд идёт до Оде́ссы. *The train is going to Odessa.*
  Без са́хара *without sugar*
  У меня́ (есть) … *I have …* (lit. *In the possession of me there is …*)
- **к** *towards*, **по** *along* + **dative**
  к музе́ю *towards the museum*
  по у́лице *along the street*
- **с** *with* + **instrumental**
  чай с молоко́м *tea with milk*
- **в** *in/at*, **на** *on/at* + **prepositional**
  Я живу́ в Москве́. (f) *I live in Moscow.*
  сарди́ны в ма́сле (n) *sardines in oil*
  на второ́м этаже́ (m) *on the 1ˢᵗ* (lit. *2ⁿᵈ*) *floor*

numbers

In English, the number *one* is followed by a singular noun while all higher numbers are followed by a plural noun: *one car, two cars, 50 cars*. The Russian numbering system works differently.

One is followed by a singular noun in the nominative case, and has different forms depending on the gender of the noun.

m	**оди́н рубль**	*one rouble*
f	**одна́ мину́та**	*one minute*
n	**одно́ ме́сто**	*one place*

Two **два**, *three* **три**, and *four* **четы́ре** are followed by a genitive singular noun:

два рубля́ *two roubles*; три мину́ты *three minutes*; четы́ре ме́ста *four places*

две, the feminine form of **два**, is used with feminine nouns:

две мину́ты *two minutes*; две сестры́ *two sisters*

Five **пять**, *six* **шесть** and higher numbers are followed by a genitive plural noun:

де́сять рубле́й *ten roubles*; сто рубле́й *a hundred roubles*
пять мину́т *five minutes*; два́дцать мину́т *twenty minutes*

Compound numbers follow the same system, i.e. *21, 31* etc. are followed by a nominative singular while *22, 32* etc. are followed by a genitive singular:

два́дцать оди́н час *21 hours*; три́дцать две мину́ты
32 minutes; сто шесть рубле́й *106 roubles*.

verbs

The infinitive of most Russian verbs ends in **-ть** preceded by a vowel. The majority of verbs end **-ать**, **-еть**, or **-ить**, but you might occasionally come across verbs ending in **-ять**, **-ыть**, **-уть**, or, very rarely, **-оть**. This is the form that you find in the dictionary, and is the equivalent of the English *to*: **знать** *to know*, **смотре́ть** *to look at*, **говори́ть** *to talk/speak*, **быть** *to be*. There are a handful of exceptions: **идти́** *to go*, **есть** *to eat* (not to be confused with **есть** *there is/are*).

present tense

The present tense indicates that the action is happening at the present time, conveying the English *I live*, *I am living*, or *I do live*. There are two sets of verb endings in Russian, based either on the letter **e**, which appears in most persons, or **и**.

	set 1	set 2
я	**у** or **ю***	**ю**
ты	**ешь / ёшь** if stressed	**ишь**
он она́ оно́	**ет / ёт** if stressed	**ит**
мы	**ем / ём** if stressed	**им**
вы	**ете / ёте** if stressed	**ите**
они́	**ут** or **ют***	**ят**

***у** after a consonant; **ю** after a vowel or soft sign

You cannot tell from the infinitive which endings the verb will take.

The first group of verbs is split into two types:

1a знать *to know*

When you remove the **-ть** ending, you're left with the verb stem **зна**, to which you add the other endings:

я	зна́**ю**	*I know*
ты	зна́**ешь**	*you know*
он она́ оно́	зна́**ет**	*he/she/it knows*
мы	зна́**ем**	*we know*
вы	зна́**ете**	*you know*
они́	зна́**ют**	*they know*

A very large number of verbs behave in the same way as **знать**, e.g. **понимáть** to understand, **слýшать** to listen to, **дéлать** to do/make:

я понимáю I understand; **онá слýшает** she listens/is listening; **мы знáем** we know; **они дéлают** they do/are doing

1b This group of verbs take the same endings as above, but the stem may differ from the infinitive:

	жить to live	**идти́** to go	**пить** to drink	**рекомендовáть** to recommend
я	живý	идý	пью	рекомендýю
ты	живёшь	идёшь	пьёшь	рекомендýешь
он онá онó	живёт	идёт	пьёт	рекомендýет
мы	живём	идём	пьём	рекомендýем
вы	живёте	идёте	пьёте	рекомендýете
они	живýт	идýт	пьют	рекомендýют

There is no way of knowing what the stem will be – it just has to be learnt. **Звать** to be called is in this group: **Меня́ зовýт …** My name is …, which literally means They call me …

Verbs in Group 2 include **говори́ть** to talk/speak, **смотрéть** to look at, **плати́ть** to pay, **стóить** to cost, **отходи́ть** to leave (of a train), **выходи́ть** to get off (a vehicle).

я	говорю́
ты	говори́шь
он онá онó	говори́т
мы	говори́м
вы	говори́те
они	говоря́т

он смóтрит he looks at/is looking at; **вы плáтите** you pay/are paying; **э́то стóит** this costs

irregular verbs

There are a handful of verbs that don't follow the examples above, e.g. **хотéть** to want, where the stem is different in the singular and plural, the endings don't follow one of the two patterns above and the stress is erratic.

я	хочу́
ты	хо́чешь
он она́ оно́	хо́чет
мы	хоти́м
вы	хоти́те
они́	хотя́т

imperative

The imperative form of the verb is used to tell people what to do. When talking to more than one person or someone you don't know well, the ending is **йте** for most verbs, while the majority of verbs in the **знать** group and a few others end in **айте**:

повтори́те *repeat*; **Повтори́те пожа́луйста.** *Repeat, please.*
скажи́те *tell*; **скажи́те мне …** *Tell me …*
говори́те ме́дленно. *Speak slowly.*
иди́те *go*; **Иди́те пря́мо.** *Go straight on.*
Да́йте мне … *Give me …*

talking about the past

The Russian past tense changes according to gender and number, not person (*I*, *you*, etc.). You simply take **ть** off the infinitive and add **-л** for masculine singular, **-ла** for feminine singular, **-ло** for neuter singular and **-ли** for the plural.

This conveys the English *ate* and *have eaten, booked/have booked*, etc.

Я заказа́л но́мер. *I booked a room.* (man speaking)
Он заказа́л но́мер. *He booked a room.*
Я заказа́ла но́мер. *I booked a room.* (woman speaking)
Она́ заказа́ла но́мер. *She booked a room.*
Мы заказа́ли такси́. *We ordered a taxi.*
Вы заказа́ли такси́. *You ordered a taxi.*
Они́ заказа́ли такси́. *They ordered a taxi.*

asking questions

Russian does not use extra words like *do* or *does*. Intonation alone indicates that you're asking a yes/no question.

Ива́н ру́сский. *Ivan is Russian.*
Ива́н ру́сский? *Is Ivan Russian?*

A question word or phrase (**что** *what*; **где** *where*; **куда́** *where to*; **когда́** *when*; **в кото́ром часу́** *at what time*; **ско́лько** *how much*) can be used to ask an open question. It has no effect on word order:

вы де́лаете *you are doing*; **Что вы де́лаете?** *What are you doing?*
ты живёшь *you live*; **Где ты живёшь?** *Where do you live?*

negatives

Do or *does* are not used in negatives either. To negate a verb, noun, adjective, or adverb, you use **не**.

Я понима́ю. *I understand*. **Я не понима́ю.** *I don't understand*.
Э́то хорошо́. *It's good*. **Э́то не хорошо́.** *It's not good*.

to be

There is no present tense of the verb *to be* (*am, is, are*) in Russian, except for the **есть** form, which means *there is* or *there are* (as well as *I have, you have*, etc. – see below). In Russian you simply omit the verb; it is understood from the context.

Я студе́нтка. *I am a student*. (lit. *I student*.)
Э́то мой муж. *This is my husband*. (lit. *This my husband*.)
Ива́н жена́т? *Is Ivan married?* (lit. *Ivan married?*)
В гости́нице есть бассе́йн. *There's a swimming pool in the hotel*.

to have

To convey the English *I have, you have*, etc. you use the phrases **у меня́ есть** and **у вас есть**, which roughly mean *in my possession there is* and *in your possession there is*. **Есть** is followed by the nominative case.

У меня́ есть брат. *I've got a brother*.
У вас есть пи́во? *Have you got any beer?*
У неё есть ка́рта. *She's got a map*.

The negative of **есть** is **нет**, *I haven't got, you haven't got* etc., which is a contraction of **не** + **есть**. **Нет** is followed by the genitive case:

У меня́ нет бра́та. *I haven't got a brother*.
У нас нет пи́ва. *We haven't any beer*.
У неё нет ка́рты. *She hasn't got a map*.

saying what you like and don't like

Нра́виться *to like* belongs in verb group 2. The particle **ся**, which means *myself, itself, oneself* etc, is tagged on after the verb ending. The Russian equivalent of *I like x* is *x likes itself to me; I like xx* is *xx like themselves to me*. Therefore the verb ending agrees with x or xx. The person or pronoun goes into the dative case:

Мне нра́вится икра́. *I like caviar*.

Мне нра́вятся традицио́нные блю́да. *I like traditional dishes.*
Тебе нра́вится моро́женое? *Do you like ice cream?*
Вам нра́вятся ру́сские фи́льмы? *Do you like Russian films?*
Мне не нра́вится икра́. *I don't like caviar.*

impersonal expressions

Often, where English uses a verb, Russian uses a phrase such as *is it possible* or *it is necessary*, followed by an infinitive:

<u>Мо́жно</u> посмотре́ть? *Can/May I/we have a look?* (lit. *Is it possible to have a look?*)

Где <u>на́до</u> выходи́ть? *Where do I/we have to get off?* (lit. *Where is it necessary to get off?*) **На́до** also translates the English *need to*, *must* and *have to*.

<u>Мо́жно</u> заказа́ть такси́. *I/you/we can/It's possible to order a taxi.*

<u>На́до</u> купи́ть биле́т. *You/we need to buy a ticket.* (lit. *It is necessary to buy a ticket.*)

Be aware that if you look up a Russian verb in the dictionary you will see it has two infinitives. Russian has what is called an aspect system and there are two aspects of every verb, perfective and imperfective, from the Latin words for *complete* or *incomplete* respectively. That means that for every one English infinitive, there are two Russian infinitives, one perfective, which you use to show that the action is complete or where the result of the action is important (in the future as well as the past, e.g. *I went to Moscow*; *I will arrive at nine o'clock*) and the other imperfective, which shows that an action is not complete or that it is the action not the result that is important (e.g. *I am reading a book*; *It was raining*).

top ten essentials

1 Describing and commenting:
   Это хорошо It's good; **Это русские** These are Russian;
   Это не далеко It's not far.

2 Talking about what's available:
   Есть бассейн There's a pool; **Есть магазины** There are shops;
   Есть кафе? Is there a café?; **Нет ресторана/ресторанов**
   There is/are no restaurant(s).

3 Talking about having:
   У меня есть сын. I have a son.
   У вас есть свободный номер? Do you have a free room?
   У нас есть традиционные сувениры. We've got traditional souvenirs.
   У нас нет икры. We haven't got any caviar.

4 Asking what things are:
   Что это? What is it?/What is this?
   Как сказать ... по-русски? How do you say ... in Russian?

5 Asking where things are:
   Где метро? Where is the metro?
   Где туалеты? Where are the toilets?

6 Asking for things:
   Дайте, пожалуйста, меню. Give me/us a menu, please. (lit. give menu)
   Дайте (мне) матрёшку. Give me the set of dolls.

7 Saying or asking if you can:
   Можно посмотреть? Can I/we/Is it possible to have a look?
   Можно. Yes, I/we/you can/it's possible.

8 Asking if you have to or need to do something:
   Простите, пожалуйста, надо купить билет? Excuse me please, do
   I/we have to buy a ticket?/Is it necessary to buy a ticket?
   Когда надо выходить? When do I/we need to get off?

9 Asking somebody to do something:
   Говорите, пожалуйста, медленно. Speak slowly please.
   Повторите, пожалуйста. Please could you say that again?
   ... я не понимаю. I don't understand.

10 Saying what you like:
   Мне нравится русское мороженое. I like Russian ice cream.
   Мне нравятся блины. I like pancakes.

Russian–English glossary

This glossary contains only those words and phrases, and their meanings, as they occur in **Talk Russian**. Parts of verbs are also given in the form in which they occur, usually followed by the infinitive in brackets.

А

а but, and
а́виа airmail
австрали́ец Australian
Австра́лия Australia
автобус bus: автобусом by bus
автомоби́ль (m) car
администра́тор administrator, manager
Аме́рика America: в Аме́рику to America
америка́нец American (m)
америка́нка American (f)
англича́нин English (m)
англича́нка English (f)
А́нглия England
анке́та registration form
аппети́т appetite: Прия́тного аппети́та! Enjoy your meal!
апте́ка chemist
аспири́н aspirin
ата́ка attack
а́том atom
аэропо́рт airport

Бб

ба́бушка grandmother
банк bank
бар bar
ба́рмен barman
бассе́йн swimming pool
бато́н loaf
без without
бе́лое white
Белору́ссия Belarus
бефстро́ганов beef stroganoff
библиоте́ка library
биле́т ticket

бифште́кс beefsteak: бифште́кс натура́льный grilled beefsteak
блины́ pancakes
блю́да dishes, courses
Болга́рия Bulgaria
бо́льше more, bigger: мне бо́льше нра́вится I prefer
борщ beetroot soup
бра́во bravo, well done
брат brother
брита́нец British (m)
Брита́ния Britain
(вы) бу́дете (быть) (you) will be
(я) бу́ду (быть) (I) will be
бульва́р boulevard
бульо́н clear soup
буфе́т snackbar, buffet
бюро́ office, desk: спра́вочное бюро́ enquiry desk, information office

Вв

в, во in, into: в оди́н коне́ц single (ticket)
вам (to) you (formal): вам нра́вится? do you like?
Ванку́вер Vancouver
ва́нна bath: с ва́нной with a bath
варе́нье jam: с варе́ньем with jam
вас you (formal): как вас зову́т? what's your name?; у вас есть? have you got?
ваш (m), ва́ша (f), ва́ше (n) your (formal)

винегре́т vegetable salad
вино́ wine
ви́ски whisky
вку́сно tasty
вода́ water
во́дка vodka
вокза́л station
Волгогра́д Volgograd
воскресе́нье Sunday
вот here, here is/are
всё all, everything
вто́рник Tuesday
второ́й (m), втора́я (f), второ́е (n) second: второ́е second (main) course; вторы́е блю́да second courses; на второ́м этаже́ on the 2nd floor
вы you (formal)
выходи́ть to get off
выходно́й день (m) closing day, day off

Гг

газ gas: без га́за still (water); с га́зом sparkling (water)
газе́та newspaper
галере́я gallery
гарни́р garnish: с гарни́ром garnished, with vegetables
где where
Герма́ния Germany
гид guide
говори́те (говори́ть) speak
го́род town
горя́чий hot: горя́чие блю́да hot dishes
гости́ница hotel

грамм gram(me)
Гре́ция Greece
грибы́ mushrooms:
с гриба́ми with
mushrooms
Гру́зия Georgia
гуля́ш goulash
ГУМ GUM (Moscow
department store)

Дд
да yes
да́йте (дава́ть) give
далеко́ far
да́ма lady
два (m/n), две (f) two
две́ри doors
двухме́стный double
(room)
де́вушка waitress, girl
де́душка (m) grandfather
дела́ things; как у вас
дела́? how are you?
(formal)
де́лать to do, make:
де́лать переса́дку to
change (trains)
день (m) day: на
ско́лько дней? for how
many days?; на два дня
for two days
десе́рт dessert
де́ти children
джин gin
дипло́м diploma
до to, up to, as far as
до свида́ния goodbye
до́лларами with dollars
дом house
дорого́й (m), дорога́я
(f), дорого́е (n) dear
дочь (f) daughter
друг friend (m)
душ shower: с ду́шем
with a shower
дя́дя (m) uncle

Ее
его́ him: как его́ зову́т?
what's his name?; у него́
есть he has
её her: как её зову́т?
what's her name?; у неё
есть she has
есть there is
есть to eat
ещё more, still: что ещё?
anything else?

Жж
жа́реный (m), жа́реная
(f), жа́реное (n) fried,
roasted
жена́ wife
жена́т (formal), жена́ты
(informal) married (man)
жест gesture
(вы) живёте (жить)
(you) live (formal) (ты)
живёшь (жить)
(you) live (informal)
(я) живу́ (жить) (I) live,
stay

Зз
заказа́ть to book: я
заказа́л (m), я заказа́ла
(f) I've booked
закрыва́ются
(закрыва́ться) (they)
close, shut: две́ри
закрыва́ются the doors
are closing
закры́т (m), закры́та (f),
закры́то (n) closed, shut
заку́ски starters,
appetizers
за́мужем (f) married
(woman)
здесь here
здра́вствуй hello
(informal); здра́вствуйте
hello (formal)
(я) зна́ю (знать) (I) know
зову́т (звать) (they) call:

как вас зову́т? what's
your name?

Ии
и and
идёт (идти́) (it) goes
иди́те (идти́) (you –
formal or pl) go
икра́ caviar
и́ли or
инжене́р engineer
информа́ция information
Ирла́ндия Ireland
Испа́ния Spain
ита́к so
Ита́лия Italy

Кк
как how
како́й? (m), кака́я? (f),
како́е? (n) каки́е? (pl)
which?; на како́м этаже́?
on which floor?
Кана́да Canada
кана́дец (m) Canadian
Ка́нберра Canberra
карп carp
ка́рта map, card: креди́
тной ка́ртой by credit
card
карто́фель (m) potatoes:
с карто́фелем with
potatoes
ка́сса cash desk
кафе́ café
кварти́ра flat
квас soft drink made
from black bread and
yeast
Ки́ев Kiev
килогра́мм kilogram(me)
киломе́тр kilometre
кино́ cinema
кио́ск kiosk
ключ key
когда́ when
колбаса́ sausage (salami)

коли́чество number, amount
ко́ма coma
коме́та comet
кому́ to whom
коне́ц end: в оди́н коне́ц single (ticket)
коне́чно of course
контро́льная рабо́та checkpoint
конце́рт concert
конья́к cognac, brandy
копе́йка kopeck
кото́рый? (m), кото́рая? (f), кото́рое? (n) which?, what? в кото́ром часу́? (at) what time?
ко́фе coffee
краси́вый (m) beautiful
кра́сный (m), кра́сная (f), кра́сное (n) red
креди́тной ка́ртой with a/by credit card
Кремль (m) Kremlin
куда́? where (to)?
купи́ть to buy
ку́рица chicken
курс course
ку́хня cooking

Лл
лимо́н lemon: с лимо́ном with lemon
лимона́д lemonade
литр litre
лифт lift, elevator
ло́жки spoons
Ло́ндон London
люкс luxury

Мм
магази́н shop
ма́ма mum, mummy
Манче́стер Manchester
ма́рка stamp: почто́вая марка postage stamp
ма́сло oil, butter: в ма́сле in oil

матрёшка set of Russian dolls
матч match (sport)
мать (f) mother
ме́дленно slowly
меню́ menu
меня́ me
у меня́ есть I have
меня́ зову́т my name is
ме́сто place
метрдоте́ль (m) head waiter
метро́ metro, underground
минера́льная вода́ mineral water
Минск Minsk
мину́та minute
мне (to) me: да́йте мне give me
мо́жно it's possible, yes, you may, OK
мой (m), моя́ (f), моё (n) my
молодо́й (m), молода́я (f), молодо́е (n) young: молодо́й челове́к waiter
молоко́ milk: с молоко́м with milk; без молока́ without milk
моро́женое ice cream
Москва́ Moscow
москви́ч (m) москви́чка (f) Muscovite
муж husband
музе́й museum
мя́со meat

Нн
на on, to, for
на́до it's necessary
нале́во (to the) left
напи́тки drinks
напра́во (to the) right
натура́льный (m), натура́льная (f), натура́льное (n) natural: бифште́кс натура́льный

grilled beefsteak
национа́льный (m), национа́льная (f), национа́льное (n), national: национа́льные блю́да national dishes
не not
него́ him: у него́ есть he has
недалеко́ not far
неё her: у неё есть she has
нет no, there isn't, there aren't
ничего́ nothing, never mind, not bad
Но́вгород Novgorod
но́мер room, number, size, size
норма́льно normally: всё норма́льно? is everything all right?
нра́вится (нра́виться) like: мне нра́вится I like (it); мне нра́вятся I like (them)
Нью-Йо́рк New York

Оо
обра́тно back: туда́ и обра́тно return (ticket)
объе́кт object
Оде́сса Odessa
оди́н (m), одна́ (f), одно́ (n) one
одноме́стный (m) single (room)
он he, it (m)
она́ she, it (f)
они́ they
оно́ it (n)
оплати́ть to pay
орке́стр orchestra, live band
остано́вка stop (bus, tram)
осторо́жно take care, be careful

отец father
открыт (m), открыта (f), открыто (n) open
открытка postcard
отправление departure
отходит (отходить) leave
очень very

Пп

пакет packet, carton
папа dad, daddy
парк park
паспорт passport
пепси-кола coke
первый (m), первая (f), первое (n) first: первое first course; первые блюда first courses; на первом этаже on the first floor
пересадка change: делать пересадку to (make a) change (train)
пешком on foot
пиво beer
пирожки pasties, small pies: с пирожками with pasties, small pies
пить to drink
план map, plan
платите (платить) pay
платформа platform: с какой платформы? from which platform?
площадь (f) square
повторите (повторить) repeat
подруга friend (f)
поезд train
пожалуйста please, don't mention it, here you are
полкило half a kilo
помидоры tomatoes
понедельник Monday
(я) понимаю (понимать) (I) understand
пообедать to dine

по-русски in Russian
посмотреть to look (at)
потом then
почта post office
почтовая марка postage stamp
прибытие arrival
привет regards, greetings
приятного аппетита enjoy your meal
проспект avenue, boulevard
простите (простить) excuse me, sorry
прямо straight on
пятница Friday: в пятницу on Friday

Рр

работа work
рад (m), рада (f) glad, pleased
(вы) рекомендуете (рекомендовать) recommend
ресторан restaurant
рис rice: с рисом with rice
ром rum
Россия Russia: в России in Russia
рубль (m) rouble: три рубля 3 roubles, пять рублей 5 roubles
русский (m), русская (f), русское (n), русские (pl) Russian: по-русски in Russian
рыба fish
рынок market: на рынке at the market

Сс

с, со with, from
салат salad
самовар samovar
Санкт-Петербург St Petersburg

сардины sardines
сауна sauna
сахар sugar: с сахаром with sugar; без сахара without sugar
свободный free
сдача change (money returned)
сегодня today
сервис-бюро service desk
сестра sister
скажите (сказать) tell (me), excuse me
сколько? how much, how many?
сладкий (m), сладкая (f), сладкое (n) sweet
сладкое sweet course
следующий (m), следующая (f), следующее (n) next
слушаю (слушать) listen: слушаю вас at your service
сметана sour cream: в сметане in sour cream; со сметаной with sour cream
сок juice
спасибо thank you
справочное бюро enquiry office
среда Wednesday: в среду on Wednesday
станция station (metro)
стоит (стоить) costs: сколько стоит? how much does it cost?; сколько стоят? how much do they cost?
стоянка stand, rank (taxi)
студент (m), студентка (f) student
суббота Saturday: в субботу on Saturday
сувениры souvenirs
суп soup

супермáркет supermarket
сухóй (m), сухáя (f), сухóе (n) dry
схéма plan: схéма метрó plan of the metro
счёт bill
съезд congress
сын son
сыр cheese

Тт

тáкже also
таксú taxi
такт tact
талóн travel coupon, ticket
твой (m), твоя́ (f), твоё (n) your (informal)
теáтр theatre
тебé (to) you (informal): тебé нрáвится? do you like (it)?
тебя́ you (informal): как тебя́ зовýт? what's your name?
телефóн telephone
тётя aunt
тóлько only
томáт tomato sauce: в томáте in tomato sauce
томáтный tomato: томáтный сок tomato juice
торт cake
традициóнный (m), традициóнная (f), традициóнное (n) traditional: традициóнная кýхня traditional cooking
трáктор tractor
трамвáй tram
трéтий (m), трéтья (f), трéтье (n) third: на трéтьем этажé on the third floor
троллéйбус trolleybus:

троллéйбусом by trolleybus
туалéт toilet
тудá (to) there: тудá и обрáтно return (ticket)
ты you (informal)

Уу

у вас есть? have you got? (formal); Как у вас делá? How are you? (formal); угóдно: что вам угóдно? what would you like?
Узбекистáн Uzbekistan
Украúна Ukraine
ýлица street: на ýлице in the street
универмáг department store
универсáм self-service shop
университéт university
ухá fish soup
Уэ́льс Wales

Фф

фамúлия surname
фáнта Fanta, fizzy orange
фотоаппарáт camera
Фрáнция France
фрýкты fruit: с фрýктами with fruit
фýнтами with pounds (sterling)

Хх

харáктер character
хлеб bread
холóдный (m), холóдная (f), холóдное (n) cold
хорошó fine, good, well, OK
(вы) хотúте (хотéть) (you – formal) want
(ты) хóчешь (хотéть) (you – informal) want

Цц

центр centre

Чч

чай tea
час hour: в котóром часý? (at) what time?; два часá 2 o'clock; семь часóв 7 o'clock
чек receipt
человéк person, people
чёрный (m), чёрная (f) чёрное (n) black
четвéрг Thursday
что? what?

Шш

шампáнское champagne
шáпка hat, cap
шашлы́к shashlyk, kebab
шкóльница schoolgirl
Шотлáндия Scotland

Щщ

щи cabbage soup
щýка pike

Ээ

экзáмен examination
экспéрт expert
Эрмитáж The Hermitage
этáж floor, storey: на какóм этажé? on which floor?
э́то this, that, it (is)

Яя

я I
я́блоки apples

English–Russian glossary

A

administrator администра́тор
airmail а́виа
airport аэропо́рт
also та́кже
America Аме́рика; to America в Аме́рику
American америка́нец (m), америка́нка (f)
all всё
and и, а
appetizers заку́ски
apples я́блоки
arrival прибы́тие
aspirin аспири́н
atom а́том
attack ата́ка
aunt тётя
Australia Австра́лия
Australian австрали́ец (m), австрали́йка (f)
avenue проспе́кт

B

band: live band орке́стр
bank банк
bar бар
barman ба́рмен
bath ва́нна; with a bath с ва́нной
to be быть
beautiful краси́вый (m), краси́вая (f), краси́вое (n)
beef stroganoff бефстро́ганов
beefsteak бифште́кс; grilled beefsteak бифште́кс натура́льный
beer пи́во
beetroot soup борщ
Belarus Белору́ссия
bigger бо́льше
bill счёт

black чёрный (m), чёрная (f), чёрное (n)
to book заказа́ть; I've booked я заказа́л (m), я заказа́ла (f)
boulevard бульва́р, проспе́кт
brandy конья́к
bravo бра́во
bread хлеб
Britain Брита́ния
British брита́нец (m), брита́нка (f)
brother брат
buffet буфе́т
Bulgaria Болга́рия
bus авто́бус; by bus авто́бусом
butter ма́сло
to buy купи́ть

C

cabbage soup щи
café кафе́
cake торт
camera фотоаппара́т
Canada Кана́да
Canadian кана́дец (m), кана́дка (f)
Canberra Канбе́рра
cap ша́пка
car автомоби́ль (m)
card ка́рта; with a/by credit card креди́тной ка́ртой
careful осторо́жный (m), осторо́жная (f), осторо́жное (n); be careful осторо́жно
carp карп
carton паке́т
cash desk ка́сса
caviar икра́
centre центр
change (money returned)

сда́ча; (transport) переса́дка; to (make a) change (train) де́лать переса́дку
champagne шампа́нское
character хара́ктер
cheese сыр
chemist апте́ка
chicken ку́рица
children де́ти
cinema кино́, кинотеа́тр
clear soup бульо́н
to close закрыва́ться; closed закры́т (m), закры́та (f), закры́то (n)
coffee ко́фе
cognac конья́к
coke пе́пси-ко́ла
cold холо́дный (m), холо́дная (f), холо́дное (n)
coma ко́ма
comet коме́та
concert конце́рт
congress съезд
costs сто́ит (сто́ить); How much does it cost? ско́лько сто́ит?; How much do they cost? ско́лько стоя́т?
course курс
cuisine ку́хня

D

dad, daddy па́па
daughter дочь
day день (m); closing day, day off выходно́й день; for how many days? на ско́лько дней?; for two days на два дня
departure отправле́ние
desk бюро́; enquiry desk, information office спра́вочное бюро́;

service desk сéрвис-бюрó

dear дорогóй (m), дорогáя (f), дорогóе (n)

department store универмáг

dessert десéрт, слáдкое

to dine обéдать, пообéдать

diploma диплóм

dishes блюда

to do дéлать

doll: set of Russian dolls матрёшка

dollar дóллар; with dollars дóлларами

doors двéри

double (room) двухмéстный (нóмер)

drink напúток

to drink пить

dry сухóй (m), сухáя (f), сухóе (n)

E

to eat есть

else ещё; anything else? что ещё?

end конéц

engineer инженéр

England Áнглия

English англичáнин (m), англичáнка (f)

Enjoy your meal! Прия́тного аппетúта!

enquiry office спрáвочное бюрó

everything всё

examination экзáмен

excuse me простúте; (tell me) скажúте

expert экспéрт

F

far далекó; not far недалекó

father отéц

fine хорошó

first пéрвый (m), пéрвая (f), пéрвое (n); first course пéрвое

fish рыба; fish soup ухá

flat квартúра

floor этáж; on which floor? на какóм этажé?; on the ground floor на пéрвом этажé; on the first floor на вторóм этажé

foot: on foot пешкóм

France Фрáнция

free свобóдный (m), свобóдная (f), свобóдное (n)

Friday пя́тница; on Friday в пя́тницу

fried жáреный (m), жáреная, (f) жáреное (n)

friend друг (m), подрýга (f)

from с, со, из

fruit фрýкты; with fruit с фрýктами

G

gallery галерéя

garnish гарнúр; garnished, with vegetables с гарнúром

Georgia Грýзия

Germany Гермáния

gesture жест

to get off выходúть

gin джин

girl дéвушка

give (to give) дáйте (дать); give me дáйте мне

glad рад (m), рáда (f)

to go идтú

good хорóший (m), хорóшая (f), хорóшее (n)

goodbye до свидáния

goulash гуля́ш

gram(me) грамм

grandfather дéдушка

grandmother бáбушка

Greece Грéция

guide гид

H

half половúна; half a kilo полкилó

hat шáпка

to have имéть; I have y меня́ есть; have you got? у вас есть? (formal), у тебя́ есть? (informal)

he он

hello здрáвствуйте (formal); здрáвствуй (informal)

her её, неё

here здесь; here is/ are вот; here you are пожáлуйста

hermitage Эрмитáж

hi привéт

him егó, негó

hot горя́чий (m), горя́чая (f), горя́чее (n); hot dishes горя́чие блюда

hotel гостúница

hour час

house дом

how как; How are you? Как у вас делá? (formal), Как у тебя́ делá? (informal); how many? скóлько?; how much? скóлько?

husband муж

I

I я

ice cream морóженое

in, into в, во

information информáция; information office

справочное бюро
Ireland Ирландия
is: it is это
it он (m), она (f), оно (n)
Italy Италия

J
jam варенье; with jam с
вареньем
juice сок

K
kebab шашлык
key ключ
Kiev Киев
kilogram(me)
килограмм; half a kilo
полкило
kilometre километр
kiosk киоск
to know знать; I know я
знаю
kopeck копейка
Kremlin Кремль (m)

L
lady дама
leave (to) отходит
(отходить)
left (to the) налево
lemon лимон; with
lemon с лимоном
lemonade лимонад
library библиотека
lift лифт
like нравится
(нравиться); I like (it)
мне нравится; I like
(them) мне нравятся;
do you like (it)? вам
нравится? (formal), тебе
нравится? (informal)
litre литр
to live жить; (I) live (я)
живу
loaf батон
London Лондон

to look (at) посмотреть
luxury: luxury room
номер люкс

M
to make делать
manager администратор
Manchester Манчестер
map карта
market рынок; at the
market на рынке
married женат (man,
informal), женаты
(man, formal), замужем
(woman)
match (sport) матч
may: you may можно
me меня; to me мне
meat мясо
menu меню
metro метро
milk молоко; with milk с
молоком; without milk
без молока
mineral water
минеральная вода
Minsk Минск
minute минута
Monday понедельник
more больше, ещё
Moscow Москва
mother мать
mum, mummy мама
Muscovite москвич (m),
москвичка (f)
museum музей
mushrooms грибы; with
mushrooms с грибами
my мой (m), моя (f),
моё (n)

N
name имя; my name is
меня зовут; What's your
name? как вас зовут?
(formal), как тебя зовут?
(informal)

national национальный
(m), национальная
(f), национальное
(n); national dishes
национальные блюда
natural натуральный
(m), натуральная (f),
натуральное (n)
necessary: it's necessary
надо
never mind ничего
New York Нью-Йорк
newspaper газета
next следующий
(m), следующая (f),
следующее (n)
no; there isn't, there
aren't нет
normally нормально
not не; there isn't, there
aren't нет; not bad ничего
Novgorod Новгород
number количество,
номер

O
object объект
o'clock: 2 o'clock два
часа; 7 o'clock семь
часов
Odessa Одесса
of course конечно
office бюро; information
office справочное бюро
oil масло; in oil в масле
OK хорошо
on на
one один (m), одна (f),
одно (n)
only только
open открыт (m),
открыта (f), открыто (n)
or или
orange: fizzy orange drink
фанта
orchestra оркестр

P

packet пакéт
pancakes блины́
park парк
passport пáспорт
pasties пирожки́
to pay оплати́ть, плати́ть
person человéк
pike щýка
place мéсто
plan план, схéма; plan of the metro схéма метро́
platform платфóрма; from which platform? с какóй платфóрмы?
please пожáлуйста
pleased рад (m), рáда (f)
possible: it's possible мóжно
post office пóчта
postage stamp почтóвая мáрка
postcard откры́тка
potatoes картóфель (m); with potatoes с картóфелем
prefer предпочитáть; I prefer мне бóльше нрáвится

R

rank (taxi) стоя́нка
receipt чек
to recommend рекомендовáть
red крáсный (m), крáсная (f), крáсное (n)
registration form анкéта
to repeat повтори́ть; Please repeat that Повтори́те, пожáлуйста
restaurant ресторáн
return (ticket) тудá и обрáтно
rice рис; with rice с ри́сом
(to the) right напрáво
rouble рубль (m)
rum ром

Russia Росси́я; in Russia в Росси́и
Russian рýсский (m), рýсская (f), рýсское (n), рýсские (pl); in Russian по-рýсски

S

salad салáт
salami колбасá
samovar самовáр
sardines сарди́ны
Saturday суббóта; on Saturday в суббóту
sauna сáуна
sausage (salami) колбасá
schoolgirl шкóльница
Scotland Шотлáндия
second вторóй (m), вторáя (f), вторóе (n); second (main) course вторóе
service desk сéрвис-бюрó
shashlyk шашлы́к
she онá
shop магази́н
shower душ; with a shower с дýшем
to shut закрывáться; shut закры́т (m), закры́та (f), закры́то (n)
single (room) одномéстный (m) (нóмер); (ticket) в оди́н конéц
sister сестрá
size нóмер
slowly мéдленно
snackbar буфéт
so итáк
soft drink made from black bread and yeast квас
son сын
sorry, excuse me прости́те (прости́ть)
soup суп; beetroot soup

борщ; cabbage soup щи; clear soup бульóн; fish soup ухá
sour cream сметáна; in sour cream в сметáне; with sour cream со сметáной
souvenirs сувени́ры
Spain Испáния
sparkling (water) с гáзом
speak (to) говори́те (говори́ть)
spoons лóжки
square плóщадь (f)
St Petersburg Санкт-Петербýрг
stamp мáрка; postage stamp почтóвая мáрка
stand, rank (taxi) стоя́нка
starters закýски
station вокзáл; (metro) стáнция
to stay жить; I stay я живý
still ещё; (water) без гáза
stop (bus, tram) останóвка
storey этáж
straight on пря́мо
street ýлица; in the street на ýлице
student студéнт (m), студéнтка (f)
sugar сáхар; with sugar с сáхаром; without sugar без сáхара
Sunday воскресéнье
supermarket супермáркет, универсáм
surname фами́лия
sweet слáдкий (m), слáдкая (f), слáдкое (n); sweet course, dessert слáдкое
swimming pool бассéйн

T

tact такт
tasty вку́сно
taxi такси́
tea чай
telephone телефо́н
tell me скажи́те
test контро́льная
рабо́та
thank you спаси́бо
that э́то, то
theatre теа́тр
then пото́м
there там; (to) there
туда́; there is есть
they они́
third тре́тий (m), тре́тья
(f), тре́тье (n)
this э́то
Thursday четве́рг
ticket биле́т, тало́н;
single ticket в оди́н
коне́ц
time: (at) what time? в
кото́ром часу́?
to (up to, as far as) до
today сего́дня
toilet туале́т
tomato тома́тный;
tomato juice тома́тный
сок; tomato sauce тома́т,
тома́тный со́ус; in
tomato sauce в тома́те
town го́род
tractor тра́ктор

traditional
традицио́нный (m),
традицио́нная (f),
традицио́нное (n);
traditional cooking
традицио́нная ку́хня
train по́езд
tram трамва́й
travel coupon тало́н
trolleybus тролле́йбус;
by trolleybus
тролле́йбусом
Tuesday вто́рник
two два (m/n), две (f)

U

Ukraine Украи́на
uncle дя́дя
underground метро́
to understand понима́ть;
I understand я понима́ю
university университе́т
Uzbekistan Узбекиста́н

V

Vancouver Ванку́вер
vegetable salad винегре́т
very о́чень
vodka во́дка
Volgograd Волгогра́д

W

waiter молодо́й челове́к
Wales Уэ́льс
to want хоте́ть

water вода́
Wednesday среда́; on
Wednesday в сре́ду
well хорошо́
well done бра́во
what? что?; (+ noun)
кото́рый? (m), кото́рая?
(f), кото́рое? (n)
when когда́
where где
where (to)? куда́?
which? како́й? (m),
кака́я? (f), како́е? (n),
каки́е? (pl)
whisky ви́ски
white бе́лый (m), бе́лая
(f), бе́лое (n)
wife жена́
wine вино́
with с, со
without без
(to) whom кому́
work рабо́та

Y

yes да
you (formal) вы,
(informal) ты
young молодо́й (m),
молода́я (f),
молодо́е (n)
your (formal) ваш (m),
ва́ша (f), ва́ше (n);
(informal) твой (m), твоя́
(f), твоё (n)